MW01504288

Understanding Healthcare Consumerism

Practical Strategies and Actionable Insights

To Your Health

Ronald E. Bachman

Ronald E. Bachman FSA, MAAA, CHC
President & CEO
Healthcare Visions, Inc.

Forward

"Understanding Healthcare Consumerism" is a compilation of proven processes, practical tools, credible resources, helpful worksheets, creative ideas, and short videos from over 35 years as an actuary, teacher and healthcare consultant at a major global consulting firm. I have taught classes on Healthcare Consumerism and consulted with small and large employer plans (including Fortune 100 companies), national insurers, technology vendors, regional HMOs, hospitals, physician groups, and other stakeholders who sit around the healthcare table. I have presented several times before Congress, testified in over 30 states, and assisted multiple government agencies regarding health reform and new legislation.

Most of you reading this book have been struggling for years to keep up with the changes in healthcare legislation, regulations, compliance, and litigation. With a focus on practical solutions, actionable strategies, and benefit designs this book will provide a perspective on where we have been, where we are, and where we are going. It will show the exciting evolution of Healthcare Consumerism. You can follow along and even anticipate the next iterative process of change and adoption. You can look into the crystal ball and see early stage products and services, new technologies, and social changes that are coming at a rapid pace to healthcare.

Brokers and consultants want new ideas that lower premiums for their clients and policyholders. Benefit managers simply want to purchase value based health and healthcare products and services. Plan members want policies that are simple and understandable. Patients want affordability, convenience and quick access to care. Care providers want to offer new cures and lower prices, but are often overloaded with paper work, limited by stifling regulations, and controlled by third party restrictions. Politicians argue over government control of healthcare.

Healthcare Consumerism also leads to "Patient-Centered" care which starts with personal responsibility and leads us from today's concerns about health and healthcare to a fulfilling life with productive longevity.

The thrust of this book is how to benefit from the rise of Healthcare Consumerism and the consumerism megatrends underway.

The basic goal of Healthcare Consumerism (HC) is to minimize the cost of healthcare by:

1. Keeping people healthy through prevention, wellness, early intervention, and well-being.
2. Minimizing accidents through safety awareness and prevention.
3. Stabilizing those with chronic and persistent health conditions through clinical services, educational support, and lifestyle changes.

HC will not benefit those who are unhealthy and don't care to get healthy. Those individuals will have higher premiums, pay more in plan cost-sharing, or at least fail to engage the healthcare delivery system effectively.

There are many dimensions and benefits to HC. One effect is to minimize third party insurance costs and maximize savings for health care expenses. Another is maximizing individual consumer control and improving the patient-provider relationship. HC opens up a new avenue of promoting healthy holistic lifestyles that extends health as a part of human capital.

Who will benefit from this book and its many moving parts? Answer: Anyone interested in the megatrend of Healthcare Consumerism and how it will affect your success as a patient, provider, employer, or a buyer or seller of health and healthcare services. Below is a brief encouragement for potential readers.

If you are an Individual – this book is for you, the healthcare consumer. You will find answers to what you can do to optimize the value of your purchases. Whether you are seeking to understand the options under your employer's group plan or selecting individual coverage, this book will help you move beyond immediate health concerns to understanding how to live a long productive life.

If you are a Consultant, Agent or Broker – this book will show you how to market, consult, and sell Healthcare Consumerism designs that will lower premiums (and future premium increases), increase coverage choices, add care convenience, and improve your clients' access to doctors, hospitals, and other medical providers.

If you are a Human Resources executive – this book will illustrate how to develop a health and healthcare strategic plan unique to your organization. This book will assist you in learning whether or not your organization is ready for change and what other organizational changes will lower health and healthcare costs of your employees.

If you are a Benefit Manager, Wellness or Communications Director – we will define and explain the pros and cons of Healthcare Consumerism. We will show how benefits interact with the development of human capital. We will explain how work effects health and how health effects work.

If you are a Solution Provider – you will see where your product fits into the rapidly evolving market of new technologies and services. You will better understand how to discuss your product/service in the language of your prospects and customers. You will see the spectrum of developing generations of Healthcare Consumerism and where your products fit into the present and future of health and healthcare.

If you are a Care Provider – you will understand how your services interact with savings options and insurance, plan design, and patient care. You will better grasp the possibilities and importance of patient involvement and engagement in wellness, well-being, treatment plans, and compliance. You will see how you can strengthen the patient-provider relationship to improve patient compliance with treatment plans.

If you are an Attorney, Legal Advisor, or Compliance Officer - We will provide examples and an understanding of the need for your services at each of the four points of any reform (legislation, regulation, compliance, and litigation).

If you are an elected official – this book will provide simplified insights into real market-based solutions. You will better understand how legislation can encourage or discourage free-market developments. You may be in a position to offer new legislation that will impact the evolution of Healthcare Consumerism and prevent the old saying, "Legislation tends to crowd out the future."

This book is a quick and easy read, but there is much more for the serious reader who wants to become an expert on Healthcare Consumerism. If you are reading this video-text in electronic form, the videos are a simple click on the "video options."

If you are reading this book in paper copy, you will need to access the internet through your PC, iPad, iphone, or other mobile device. You will find all of the videos at www.hcbookvideos.com or read the QR Code located below and at the end of each chapter with your phone and QR code reader app (A free download at your app store).

You may also want to explore more information, laws, and regulations on health reform and Healthcare Consumerism at www.ihcuniversity.com

CONTENTS

ACKNOWLEDGMENTS

This is the first book I have ever written, so it is hard to limit the acknowledgements to a short list. The thoughts, the ability, encouragement, and the ideas in this book have been generated by many people over my 35 year career as an actuary and healthcare consultant. Some trained me as an actuarial technician. Some taught me to think outside the box. Others inspired me with their creative approaches to problem solving. Some challenged me to see the big picture and industry megatrends.

Experts have provided me insight to legal, regulatory, and medical issues. Many have supported my passions for healthcare and politics. Most bosses believed in me and gave me confidence to seek out new ideas and hire exceptional staff. The most important people have been the friends and associates who worked with me over several careers and turned work into fun.

I have always had two skills that that benefited me the most over the years: (1) an insight to grasp good ideas and thoughts of others and (2) an innate ability to simplify complicated thoughts and ideas into text and visual formats. As Laurie Greiner of Shark Tank says, "I can immediately recognize a hero from a zero." This book is a composite of the many ideas, inspirations, and creative concepts others have discussed or alluded to previously. I have simply put it all together in a logical easy to understand format.

The best way for me to say thank you to so many key folks that have significantly influenced my work and my thinking is to list them by name and the place in my career in which our paths crossed. Many have no idea how much they have meant to me. Some may not even remember me, but they all have had a profound influence on me.

Kennesaw Life Insurance Company:
Frank Lackey FSA, Ray Biscoglia FSA
Life of Georgia:
Richard Wolf FSA, Roy Day, Jim Brooks FSA, Harold Cohen FSA,
David Stonecipher FSA, Jack Bragg FSA
MILICO:
Bob Whitney FSA, Joey Moskowitz FSA, Art Williams,
Bo Adams
Field Media:
Doug Field CEO
Georgia Public Policy Foundation:
Kelly McCutcheon, Benita Dodd, Judson Hill JD
Center for Health Transformation
Speaker Newt Gingrich, Nancy Desmond, Jim Frogue
PricewaterhouseCoopers:
Team Mates: Frank Raiti, Reed Keller, Don Weber, Bob Sears,
Claudette Duncan, Claude Carruth CPA, Ken Berklee,
David Chin MD, Steve Gerst MD, Tim Ray, Harold Dankner,
Ron Finch PhD, Mike Thompson FSA, Lee Launer FSA,
Terrance Fowler CPA, Mike Cadger, Stephany Kong MD,
Tania Malik JD, Rick Irwin FSA, Tony Holmes FSA.
Clients::
Bob Hallock CEO, Eric Norwood CEO, Tom Crawford, Cecily
Hall, David Harrell CEO, Marilyn Richmond, Doug
Walter, Henry Englicka
Pioneers and Thought Leaders in Healthcare:
Pat Rooney, John Goodman PhD, Tony Miller, Bill Thomas,
Mike Showalter, Phil Micali, John Hickman JD, Bill
Sweetnam JD, Roy Ramthun, John Young, Lyle Miller PhD,
Doug Bulleit, Jon Comola, Tom Johnson CEO,
Wendy Lynch PhD, Jack Curtis CEO, Jim Pshock CEO

I could not have been more blessed to work with such qualified professionals. Of course, the folks in the trenches at each of the organizations facilitated my work efforts and to all of them I give a heartfelt thank you.

Last but certainly not least is my family support. Daughter Marian Chase helped to edit and wife Beverly supported my hours of research and writing.

Introduction

Wanting good health is not enough. We are typically American. We want to be paid to do the right things. Who would have taken out the garbage as youths, or done household chores without an allowance? With Healthcare Consumerism (HC), plan members can be financially rewarded for doing the right activities that improve their health and save money.

If just wanting good health was enough we wouldn't have the avoidable health problems that exist. We still have too many smokers, and Type II diabetes is a national epidemic. Rewards can be based on activities such as participation in a wellness assessment, compliance with a condition management program (e.g. taking medications, diet, exercise, keeping office visits), completion of annual physicals, and maintenance of good health characteristics (e.g. blood pressure, cholesterol, nicotine use, body mass index).

The transformation to Healthcare Consumerism is well underway. It is a consolidation of proven successful ideas in the marketplace. As a combination of ideas it is a new way to save lives, improve health, and lower costs. Numerous studies indicate that early adopters of HC designed plans saw positive results from the greater use of preventive care services and lower year over year healthcare cost increases. Developing iterations and the newer forms of HC products and services are rapidly evolving to meet the broader demands of the marketplace.

Many criticized 1st generation plans, sometimes referred to as Consumer Directed Healthcare Plans (CDHP). They seemed to only benefit the young, healthy, and wealthy. Those concerns were mitigated as CDHPs evolved beyond the 1st generation plans to more sustainable and effective future generations of Healthcare Consumerism.

HC is much more than employers implementing high deductible Consumer-Directed Healthcare Plans with attached saving accounts. The future is about empowering individuals with information and financial responsibility that supports a position of ownership. It's about supporting and rewarding healthy behaviors regardless of plan design. It's about engaging employees, employers, providers, carriers, and other stakeholders in a new relationship that deals with health and healthcare rather than sickness and disease.

The existing health care system has a fundamental structural problem. Third-party reimbursements and the absence of individual financial responsibility foster an environment of entitlement.

Corporate benefit managers and human resource executives are searching for ways to effectively design health plans to lower costs and improve quality of care. Wellness, well-being, and prevention initiatives are being widely adopted. Disease and condition management programs are identifying chronically ill populations for targeted help. Education, communication, and incentives (and penalties) are being used to support and reinforce information on safety, healthy lifestyles, and healthy choices.

Healthcare costs continue to rise. Real change in cost and quality is not about more management, additional programs, limiting formularies, or cost shifting. Real change involves engagement, personal responsibility, a willingness to learn, and a process to alter health and healthcare purchasing behaviors.

Some of the ideas and thoughts presented in this material may seem too new for some organizations. There may be good thoughts and intentions, but decision makers may need time to socialize the impacts on their staff. There may be resistance from employees, unions, and even management. If the current old model programs are not working, remember the old saying, as Speaker Newt Gingrich often states, "REAL Change requires....REAL Change."

Chapter 1

The Movement to
Healthcare Consumerism

The world of health and healthcare is changing. When major transformations occur in history we are rarely aware of the changes until in retrospect, we see that they have become an accepted part of our culture. No one knew when the Renaissance was underway. No one announced the point at which the Soviet Union and Communism began to fail. Few understood in the 1980-90's the dramatic changes that affordable personal computers, cell phones, and the internet would have on our daily lives. It is typical that only after a pause and look back do we see the importance of specific events and their true impact.

If one listens closely you may catch the sound of a Paul Revere-like spirit signalling the clarion call that the transformation to Healthcare Consumerism in the United States is well underway.

A. From Supply Controls to Demand Controls - Video 103

Since the 1990's health insurance in the United States has gradually but relentlessly transitioned from various forms of managed care to HC.

Traditional insurance for medical care is based on a supply-control model with demand assumed to be unlimited. To lower costs plans limit access to providers and control the supply of care (e.g. it's not medically necessary, it's not available, it's not covered, you're not sick enough, you'll have to wait for that service). This "managed care" system is described by some as "Delay, Deny, and Defeat."

Rather than a "supply-control" system, the future of healthcare is based on a "demand-control" model with economic forces similar to those that affect all other consumer goods and purchasing behaviors. Clearly, health and healthcare are not the same as purchasing retail goods and services; however, certain mega trends have been impacting our economy and service industries that have a parallel in healthcare. It is the paradigm shift that is transforming the delivery and cost of health and healthcare.

Demand for care under a pure third-party reimbursement system has been proven to be uncontrollable. However, once plan members are given a financial stake in their health and healthcare decisions they tend to limit unnecessary use of services. When possible they select the least costly, most convenient, appropriate care that meets their needs.

HC is the reflection of the same forces influencing other parts of society (i.e. Facebook, LinkedIn, stock transactions, online shopping, self-checkout counters). Those megatrend forces are:

1. Personal Responsibility
2. Self-help & self-care
3. Individual Ownership
4. Portability
5 Transparency (the right to know)
6. Consumerism (empowerment)

B. Healthcare Consumerism Defined

HC is about transforming an organization's health benefit plan into one that puts economic purchasing power—and decision-making—in the hands of participants. It's about supplying the information and decision support tools they need, along with financial incentives, rewards/penalties, and other benefits that encourage personal involvement in altering health and healthcare purchasing behaviors.

HC includes a broad set of options for engaging plan members. HC embodies an approach for how employees help themselves and how they are supported by their employer and/or insurer. Developing HC concepts of personal responsibility and individual ownership for health and healthcare decisions is also affected by the overall organizational culture.

C. The Purpose and Objectives for HC - <u>Video 104</u>

If HC is to be a sustainable concept it must work for everyone. The purpose cannot be just to lower costs. It must have a more elevated goal. When done for the right reasons there is a "moral imperative" of saving lives and improving health. By focusing on better health first, the resulting cost reduction will satisfy the "economic imperative" of lowering the costs and saving jobs.

The objectives of HC are broad and all encompassing. Designed and implemented properly and with a focus on successful transformation, the objectives consist of changing participant health and healthcare purchasing behaviors by:

1. Narrowing market cost and quality variations using "patient power" to:
   a. Increase the transparency of healthcare costs to plan participants.
   b. Give plan participants more control over and "shared responsibility" for managing their own healthcare and related costs.
   c. Supply participants with the tools to act as better informed healthcare consumers.
2. Reducing Discretionary costs through informed purchasing & incentives/penalties.
3. Reducing Acute Care costs with incentivized hospital reimbursements by tiering reimbursements based upon cost and quality.

4. Reducing Chronic Care costs through improved adherence to treatments and disease/condition management programs.
5. Reducing Long Term costs with added incentives/rewards for "good health."

The other basic requirements of a good HC plan are:

1. It must be a viable option for the sickest plan members, and
2. It must protect those who are not "techies" or who don't want to research plan or care options and treatment alternatives.

Delivering on the first requirement moves HC beyond the initial CDHP plans that were selected mostly by the young and healthy. 2nd+ generation plans provide rewards/penalties and incentives for both the healthy and the unhealthy. The beneficiaries will be those who are willing to improve their health (or at least stabilize their condition) to avoid expensive hospitalizations and re-hospitalizations and to be compliant with treatment plans.

The second requirement is important because not everyone is motivated to use support tools to seek the most cost effective services. Plan members may have other more important or financially lucrative activities for their time. In any case, those individuals will pay more out of pocket and maybe get less cost effective care. However, a limited maximum out-of-pocket exposure lowers the risk to family assets, children's college funds, or financial bankruptcy.

D. HC Choices and Changing Roles – <u>Video 105</u>

HC provides plan members with decisions in the months after annual enrollment. With HC plan benefits, member premium contributions, and provider reimbursements can change during the year based upon the plan member's choices and actions to participate in reward programs, comply with medical treatments, make healthy lifestyle choices, keep to diet and exercise routines, and become an educated healthcare patient and consumer.

Among the areas of choices that could include rewards and incentives/penalties are:

    a. Wellness
    b. Preventive care
    c. Early Intervention
    d. Lifestyle Options (diet, exercise, smoking, safety)
    e. Self-help, self care (Health literacy)
    f. Discretionary Expenses (e.g. Office Visits, Diagnostic, X-ray, Lab work, Emergency Room visits, Prescription Drugs)
    g. Value purchasing (e.g. Referenced-Based Pricing, Bundled services, Outpatient vs. Inpatient Care, online services)
    h. Participation in Condition Management Programs
    i. Adherence to Medical Treatment Plans

HC does not put all of the pressure or responsibility for change on the plan member or patient. All stakeholders have new roles to play.

Plan Members

- Increased responsibility to be informed about their own health & healthcare
- Involved in their own treatment and medical necessity decisions
- Understanding alternatives and access to needed care
- Involved in financial costs of health & healthcare

Employers

- Facilitators of change
- Health Literacy: Provide increased information and decision making tools
- Improved employee morale with choice and access
- Link to productivity, absenteeism, disability, turnover
- Implement consumerism that can improve costs/budgeting (current & future)

Insurers and Self-Insured Employers

- Focus on high cost cases, diseases, and population management
- Become responsible for communications, training, education, and healthcare literacy
- Recognize that value added services may change (including financial transactions and asset management)
- Strengthen that patient-provider relationship

Providers

- More direct involvement with patients and treatment
- Service and quality will be determined by consumers
- Pricing will become more flexible and visible

Overall implications

- Roles will change for all players
- The options will change quickly - your strategies must prepare you for rapid market changes

Video 103	Video 104	Video 105

Chapter 2

Consumer Driven Healthcare Plans
Account Based Plans

A. Account-Based Plan Designs

Health Reimbursement Arrangements (HRAs) were allowed in 2002 under an existing law through a clarifying rule made by the United States Treasury. Health Savings Accounts (HSAs) were created by a new law in 2003. HSAs were established as an improved permanent form of the 1996 Medical Savings Accounts (MSAs). These are dramatic changes from the 1979 use-it-or-lose-it Flexible Spending Arrangements (FSAs).

Account based plans are subsets of HC. Legally, HRAs and HSAs are very different. They have very different funding provisions and profoundly different rules for use. The growth of companies offering HRA and HSA account-based plans is impressive, especially for larger group plans.

% of Companies with Health Benefits Offering Account-Based Plans By Size and By Year		
50-499 Employees (Small Employers)	**500+ Employees** (Large Employers)	**20,000+ Employees** (Very Large Employers)
Year		
2016 25%	61%	80%
2015 28%	59%	73%
2014 26%	48%	72%
2013 23%	39%	63%
2012 22%	36%	59%
2011 20%	32%	48%
2010 16%	23%	51%
2009 15%	20%	43%
2008 9%	20%	45%
Sources: Mercer's National Survey of Employer-Sponsored Health Plans		

B. Basic CDHP with HRA - <u>Video 112</u>

Generic Consumer-Driven Heath Plans (CDHPs) are typically high deductible health plans. (Note lower case lettering). Without an attached HRA, high deductible plans can be used to directly shift costs to employees by lowering premiums and increasing patient cost sharing at the time of medical care. However, many CDHP's include an HRA that can fill in some or most of the deductible and allow an accumulation and carryover of unused funds from year to year.

HRAs have the flexibility to be added to any plan design. However, HRAs are "notional" accounts. That is, they are "promises" by an employer to make allocations of dollars available under certain conditions. As such, they are not guaranteed funds. In addition, HRAs can only be funded by employers. Therefore, plan members cannot make tax advantaged deposits into HRAs. Note: They are "arrangements" NOT "accounts."

Under the HRA concept members receive from their employer an HRA allocation that they can use to pay for covered medical services. These allocations generally range from one-quarter to one-half of the single employee deductible (double for families). Unlike the use-it-or-lose-it FSA, the unused HRA funds can be rolled over into future years and added to the next annual HRA allocation.

If during the year the HRA fund is exhausted, the member must meet any remaining "deductible gap" before receiving insurance payments under the plan. Network discounts apply to all services regardless of whether the source of payment is the HRA, employee out-of-pocket, or plan reimbursements.

First-dollar coverage is available for preventive services such as physicals, mammograms, and well-child care. HRA funds can be used to fill in plan deductibles or for coverage of copayments. If allowed by the employer, HRAs can be used for non-plan but IRS-qualified medical expenses (those allowed under IRS code 213(d)).

HRAs can also be used to purchase other health insurance coverages (e.g., long-term care).

Below is a traditional CDHP plan design for a single employee. With extensive 100% reimbursement for certain preventive care coverages there is a greater potential for carry-over of unused funds since the cost of preventive care services will not be deducted from the HRA account.

Basic CDHP with HRA – Example		
100 % Preventive Coverage		1. 100% Preventive Care
$XXX Employer's HRA Allocation		2. Health Reimbursement Arrangement - Initial $XXX Employer Allocation & any carry-over
Potential Deductible Gap $YYY		3. $YYY Deductible Gap (Can be funded with FSA)
20% Coins to a Max OOP $ZZZ	PPO 80% Coverage	4. 20% In-Network Patient Coinsurance to a $ZZZ Maximum Coinsurance Out of Pocket 5. 40% Out–of-Network Patient Coinsurance; No Maximum Out-of-Pocket
100% Coverage		6. 100% Coverage – Unlimited $

(Dollar values for HRA, deductible, coinsurance, and the Max OOP are left generic as designs can vary from plan to plan).

C. CDHP - HSA Eligible High Deductible Health Plans

As a part of the 2003 Medicare Modernization Act, account-based options were expanded when HSA eligible High Deductible Health Plans (HDHPs) were created by new legislation. Unlike the notional values of HRAs, HSAs are real dollars put into a member controlled savings account.

HSA eligible plans are legally called <u>H</u>igh <u>D</u>eductible <u>H</u>ealth <u>P</u>lans or HDHPs. (Note: capital letters as written in the law). HSA eligible HDHP's have an attached savings option where real tax advantaged dollars may be deposited by employers, employees, and even third parties.

HSAs are triple tax advantaged. Both plan members and employers can make tax advantaged contributions to an HSA. Contributions are: (1) tax free if from employers or tax deductible deposits if by employees, (2) are tax free accumulations, and (3) are tax free when withdrawn for allowed health purposes. Unused HSAs roll-over each year and never expire. Plan members can take it with them after they leave employment and use it for future eligible medical expenses, including retirement medical costs.

In order to access the triple tax advantages of an HSA, Congress imposed strict requirements on acceptable plan designs. An HSA eligible plan has a legally prescribed minimum individual and family deductible and a maximum out-of-pocket limit. The deductibles, maximum HSA contributions, and out-of-pocket limits are inflation adjusted each year.

For policyholders and covered spouses age 55 or older, the HSA annual contribution limit includes an additional $1000 "catch-up" provision. Employers contributing to an HSA must make comparable contributions on behalf of all employees with comparable coverage. Distributions from an HSA are excludable from gross income if made for services that are for Qualified Medical Expense (QME) as defined by the U.S. Treasury.

In spite of their legal description, HDHP's do NOT have to be high cost sharing at the time of medical care. Employers can establish the plans with an initial account deposit and/or provide additional deposits after enrollment based on incentive/penalty programs and plan member actions.

While HSA eligible plans are an important step in the evolutionary process towards HC, there are two major problems stemming from the legal restrictions in the original 2003 legislation.

1.   Prescription drugs cannot be reimbursed until the full plan deductible has been satisfied either by available HSA funds or patient out-of-pocket payments. Some medications can be covered at a 100% reimbursement as "preventive care." However, it is not always clear when a drug is preventive and when it is treatment for a condition. (e.g. Are statins for preventing heart disease or for treating the diagnosis of high cholesterol?)

2.   By law, HSA eligible plans are legally prescribed plan designs with certain design features required and certain coverages prohibited. For example, they must have a minimum upfront deductible that may be larger than an employer would otherwise want to implement. In addition, HSA eligible plans cannot cover non-preventative office visits at 100%. They cannot cover any accident benefits at 100%.

Basic CDHP with HSA		
100 % Preventive Coverage		1. 100% Preventive Care
$XXX Employer's HSA Deposit		2. Health Savings Account - Employer Initial $XXX Contribution & any carry-over
$YYY Employee's HSA Deposit		3. Health Savings Account – Employee $ YYY Contribution
Potential Deductible Gap $ZZZ		4. ZZZ Potential Deductible Gap
20% Coins to a Max OOP $AAA	PPO 80% Coverage	5. 20% In-Network Patient Coinsurance to a $AAA Maximum Coinsurance Out of Pocket 6. 40% Out–of-Network Patient Coinsurance; No Maximum Out-of-Pocket
100% Coverage		7. 100% Coverage – Unlimited $

(Dollar values for HSA, deductible, coinsurance, and the MOOP are left generic as designs can vary from plan to plan)

Consider CDHPs and HSA eligible plans to be a more limited subset of HC. Both options rely mainly on the plan design to motivate and engage employees to make better health and healthcare decisions. Plans with either an initial HRA or an HSA are examples of Consumer Driven Healthcare plans that focus mainly on lowering discretionary expenses (e.g. emergency room, office visits, and prescription drugs). These concepts can be dramatically improved with incentives and penalties that are effective tools for motivating change. Each organization is unique. What motivates a unionized plan member in a manufacturing environment may be different from what motivates a millennial in the high-tech industry. There are many more options and approaches (described in later chapters) that are proving effective.

A Rand study found that when people shifted into health insurance plans with high deductibles, their health spending dropped an average of 14 percent. Healthcare spending also was lower among families enrolled in high-deductible plans that had health savings accounts.

However, companies are now moving to more creative designs and even full-replacement of traditional plans. In today's world of personalization, a one-size fits all strategy is not flexible enough for a diverse workforce.

Video 112

Chapter 3

The Healthcare Consumerism Grid

Five distinct generations of HC have been identified. It starts with a first generation model focusing on basic high deductible plans leading to products and services supporting personalized and community health and healthcare.

The HC Grid shown below is not an academic or think tank model. The grid reflects years of experience and active monitoring of changes occurring in the marketplace.

The author continues to monitor the market for a 6th generation. Appendix B identifies nascent products and services coalescing around a potential 6th generation of HC. However, new generations will not be officially added until the evidence shows a significant market adoption of sustainable new products and services.

A. Five Generations of HC–Video 110

HC is evolving at a rapid pace. The experiences from the 1st generation adopters of CDHP and HSA eligible HDHPs formed the basis for new generations, creative ideas, exciting product designs, and alternative ways to reward and incentivize or penalize plan members. Greater awareness, acceptance and uptake by employers, insurers, and a growing number of vendors are building a reservoir of thoughtful and creative new solutions to actively engage participants.

National and regional insurers have invested billions in new systems and product development. Second, third, fourth and even fifth generation products are actively and aggressively being developed.

The core concept of all five generations is how to optimize engagement of plan members in healthcare choices and healthy activities.

The Evolution of Healthcare Consumerism				
1st Generation	2nd Generation	3rd Generation	4th Generation	5th Generation
Discretionary Expenses	Behavior Changes	Health & Performance	Personalized Health	Community Health
Impact on Engagement and Cost Management				
Low............................Medium............................High				

1st **Generation HC** – The focus is on high deductible plan designs, implementation of personal care accounts (HRAs, HSAs, FSAs), and basic decision support tools.

• Impact: Health management, discretionary expenses (e.g. Office Visits, Prescription Drugs, Emergency Room visits, some diagnostic-xray-labs).

2nd **Generation HC** – The focus is on behavior changes and the use of individual and group incentives/rewards/penalties to effectively change health and healthcare purchasing behaviors.

• Impact: Chronic & Persistent Conditions, Pre-Natal care, wellness, preventive care, and early intervention.

3rd **Generation HC** – The focus is on human capital, health and organizational performance, and the integration of health, work performance, and the organization's bottom line.

• Impact: Organizational health, turnover, absenteeism, productivity, disability, impaired presenteeism, well-being, unscheduled sick days, workplace safety, creativity, and teaming.

4th Generation HC – The focus is on personalized health, lifestyle, lifecycle activities, and the impact of how behavior change affects an individual's health and healthcare.

- Impact: Lifecycle needs, personal health, genetic predispositions, predictive modelling, healthy habits, and technology disrupters.

5Th Generation HC – The focus is on connections and engagement with community, family, and friends to support healthy living.

- Impact: Productive longevity, stress management, personal safety, and caring, sharing and helping others.

It is important to recognize that each generation builds on the previous ones and plans may include aspects of multiple generations. One generation of HC does not necessarily replace the prior generation.

Furthermore, no one stakeholder (e.g. employee, employer, insurer, or provider) can advance too far into the future without the involvement and participation of the others. As such, you can expect advancement in the coming years to be an iterative process of customer demands and vendor solutions.

B. HC Building Blocks

HC has many dimensions, but five key building blocks stand out as common to most plans:

1. Personal Accounts: FSAs, HRAs, HSAs
2. Health Management: Wellness/Prevention and Early Intervention
3. Condition Management: Disease Management and Case Management Programs
4. Health Literacy: Information and Decision Support Programs
5. Incentive and Compliance Reward Programs

Each building block will be detailed in subsequent chapters. Each represents a "promise" and potential for a better future.

The Promises and Potential of Healthcare Consumerism	
Major Building Blocks	**The Promise**
Personal Care Accounts	The Promise of Demand Control & Savings
Health Management	The Promise of Well-being
Condition Management	The Promise of Health And Functionality
Health Literacy	The Promise of Understanding &Transparency
Rewards/Incentives	The Promise of Shared Savings

It is the creative development, efficient delivery, efficacy, and successful interaction of these elements that will prove the success or failure of HC.

C. The Future is HC

The future belongs to the broad concept of HC. It includes and consolidates most of the features of other concepts such as, CDHP's, HDHPs, HSA eligible plans, Patient-centered care, value purchasing, personalized healthcare, and others. It includes new ways to purchase products and services (consumerism) and new ways to use and interact with care providers (patient-centered).

HC is independent of plan design. HC includes opportunities to accumulate funds or receive other incentives through "shared-savings". HC can reward healthy choices and treatment compliance in many ways. Lower deductibles, reduced member premium contributions, and added benefits are all a part of HC.

The strength of HC is the multiple and varied ways that can be used to engage employees to create positive changes in behaviors.

The HC Grid	1st Gen	2nd Gen	3rd Gen	4th Gen	5th Gen
	Health & Discretion Expenses	Behavior Changes, Shared Savings	Integrated Health & Performance	Personal Care	Community Health & Productive Longevity
Personal Care Accounts	Initial Account Only	Activity & Compliance Rewards	Indiv. & Grp Corporate Metric Rewards	Specialized Accts, Matching HRAs, Expanded QMEs	Volunteer Vessels, Pay Forward, Charitable Giving
Wellness & Health Mgmt	100% ACA Mandated Preventive Care	Web-based Behavior Change Support	Worksite Wellness, on-site clinics, safety, Stress & Error reduction	Genomics Predictive Modelling Push Technology	Natural Resource Flows, Longevity more than Health
Disease & Condition Mgmt	Basic Info & Health Coach	Disease Specific Complying Awards	Population Mgmt, IHM, Integrated Back-to-Work	Wire-less support, Cultural DM, Holistic Care	Functionality, Community, Faith & Spirituality
Decision Support & Health Literacy	Passive Info, Discretionary Expenses, Rx, ER, D-X-L	Personal Health Mgmt, info with access incentives	Health & Perform. Info, Integrated Health & Work Data	Arrive in time info, Information therapy, Targeted messaging	Friendship Pods, Wisemen, Sharing Circles, Social networks
Incentive, Rewards, Penalties	Cash, Tickets, Gift Cards, Trinkets,	Health Incentive Accts, Activity Incentives	Non-health corporate metric driven incentives	Personal Develop. Plan Incentives, Health Status	Psychic Rewards, Recognition, Honor, Respect, Love

The above HC Grid is the "crystal ball" - a visual framework - for understanding the future generations of HC and the five major building blocks.

The overall goal of HC is to assist individuals in making more informed health and healthcare decisions which will favorably impact clinical outcomes and lower the cost of care.

We will discover the underlying details of both the building blocks and the generations in future chapters. Combining these two dimensions produces the "HC Grid."

Before we delve into the plan design and selection of HC features we need a structured approach to determine what form(s) of HC will work for any specific organization. The next few chapters provide a concrete approach for identifying those solutions unique to an organization.

Video 110

Chapter 4

Basic Principles, Vision, and Strategies
Video 101

A. Identifying Basic Principles

It is amazing how many people and organizations skip the foundational steps of building a consensus for change. Here is one way to proceed. First, gather the key decision makers (e.g. HR VP, benefit manager, wellness professional, CFO, Communications VP) in a room away from normal operations. Go off site if necessary.

Go through a few key questions (examples are shown below) to establish the organization's unique basic guiding principles. There are no right or wrong answers. The DISCUSSION that follows from the individual answers is the important part. It is critical that the discussion be open, honest, and not judgmental.

Principles are the guideposts for testing later decisions. Periodically check back to these original principles to see if decisions are consistent with the initial principles. Then, either modify the principles and priorities (what was thought to be important may have changed along the way) or review and change decisions to be consistent with the original principles.

To initiate the process, the following is a list of 31 sample principles that can help to prioritize actions. Make copies of the list below. Have all participants in the meeting mark each item with a score of 1 to 5.

While there are no right or wrong answers, not everything should be marked a 1 for "important." Require that a maximum of five items be listed as 1's and at least five items be listed as 5's. After allowing time for all participants to read and score the list, have a robust discussion of why items were picked and what they mean for the organization. No one should dominate the discussion.

#	Basic Principles	Circle Selected Rating				
		Important				Not Important
1	Have the Right Vision and Vision Statement	1	2	3	4	5
2	Have a 3-5 Year Roadmap/Strategic Plan	1	2	3	4	5
3	Consider Other Related Corporate Initiatives	1	2	3	4	5
4	Create plan as part of Employer of Choice	1	2	3	4	5
5	Consider other HR metrics	1	2	3	4	5
6	Provide Info on Rx Costs & Alternatives	1	2	3	4	5
7	Provide Info on Physician.and Medical Costs	1	2	3	4	5
8	Provide Information on Hospital Costs	1	2	3	4	5
9	Provide Info on the Quality of Physician Care	1	2	3	4	5
10	Provide Info on the Quality of Hospital Care	1	2	3	4	5
11	Focus on Discretionary Costs (Rx and ER)	1	2	3	4	5
12	Focus on High Cost Claims & Claimants	1	2	3	4	5
13	Focus on Wellness and Preventive Care	1	2	3	4	5
14	Focus on an Individual Behavior Changes	1	2	3	4	5
15.	Focus on Group Behavior Changes	1	2	3	4	5
16	Use Compliance Incentives, Rewards/Penalties	1	2	3	4	5
17.	Increase Cost sharing to Change Behaviors	1	2	3	4	5
18.	Increase Employee Contrib.to Offset Costs	1	2	3	4	5
19	Focus on Overall Plan Cost Reduction	1	2	3	4	5
20	Set the Right Metrics for Monitoring Progress	1	2	3	4	5
21	Build Broad Employee Agreement for Change	1	2	3	4	5
22	Minimize Change from Current Plans	1	2	3	4	5
23	Make Choices and Plan Options available	1	2	3	4	5
24	Improve Access to Care	1	2	3	4	5
25	Maintain Existing Network of Providers	1	2	3	4	5
26	Provide $ for post-65 retirement healthcare	1	2	3	4	5
27	Provide $ for pre-65 retirement healthcare	1	2	3	4	5
28	Provide $ for non-plan medical coverages	1	2	3	4	5
29	Provide $ for terminated Employees healthcare	1	2	3	4	5
30	Provide $ for non-healthcare expenses	1	2	3	4	5
31	Alternative to cutting benefits or increasing contributions	1	2	3	4	5

Considerate listening to others will produce the best results. Higher level officers of the organization should speak last. It is amazing how different the selections will be from person to person.

The discussion should develop a consensus around 3-5 of the most important principles. Keep discussing until the group has general agreement on 3-5 items. Keep the results for future reference in developing a vision statement. This will be a good reminder if later implementation decisions get off track.

A team recorder should take notes throughout the discussion. Key words and phrases will surface during those discussions that will make the next step - creating a vision statement - easier.

B. Creating a Vision Statement

Once there is consensus on the "basic principles" the group can move to creating a vision statement. A vision statement should be a simple and concise declaration of what the organization intends to accomplish. If the discussion of principles was robust and given appropriate time, the oft repeated words that come out of the principles discussion will likely form the basis of the vision statement.

Here are five examples from actual company initiatives working to change their health insurance benefits.

Sample Vision Statements:

1.   Providing high perf.rming highly educated employees and their families with the security of comprehensive health and healthcare coverage that meets their diverse needs and rewards their personal involvement and responsibility as wise users of services to optimize their individual health status and functionality.

2. Affect employee behavior change towards healthier lifestyles and greater consumerism through the use of rewards and incentives.

3. Make employees better consumers of healthcare services by providing them with the necessary health education, decision support tools and useful information including provider cost and quality data.

4. Encourage greater employee awareness and involvement in healthcare and financial decision making, as a building block towards a defined contribution strategy for healthcare in the future.

5. Create health and healthcare program options valued by employees that adapt effectively to environmental trends that increase the quality of services, improve access to care, and lower costs.

Now, take the time and make the effort to write a vision statement for your organization. Get the group to sign off on the vision statement. Make adjustments and word edits as needed. This is not a pedantic exercise. You will find it valuable throughout the rest of your journey to develop an effective HC approach that is unique to your organization.

C. Identifying Acceptable Strategies

Strategies are how you will carry out the vision statement based on the basic principles. Using the same group of decision makers, start with the list of fifteen below (you can add your own). Make a copy for each team member. Have each person mark each potential strategy as 1 through 5 (High Priority to Low Priority). Make sure a maximum of 2-3 are number 1's and a minimum of 2-3 are number 5's.

The discussion needs to be an open non-confrontational dialogue of individual choices. Develop a consensus set of strategies to carry out the vision. Check back to see if the strategies are consistent with your selected basic principles.

#	Acceptable Strategies	Circle Selected Rating				
		Priority				
		High				Low
1	**Create Transparency** – support "employee's right to know," minimize distortions of third-party reimbursement system, create transparency in costs, provide education & training on healthcare costs, use decision support programs.	1	2	3	4	5
2	**Create Personal Involvement** – establish greater financial involvement through HDHPs, HRAs or HSAs, reward good behavior, offer valued options, provide long term incentives, provide immediate feedback.	1	2	3	4	5
3	**Be Bold and Creative** - Shift from supply-side controls to demand-side control designs. Be an early adopter/fast follower, consider out-of-the-box ideas.	1	2	3	4	5
4	**Focus on 15-20% High Cost Population** – Provide financial protection to families in need due to high unexpected medical costs and/or chronic conditions.	1	2	3	4	5
5	**Focus on Saving Lives and Improving Health** – Focus on improving the health of the entire population regardless of plan design selected. Implement prevention & wellness for long term savings and Disease Management for immediate impact.	1	2	3	4	5
6	**Focus on Preventive Care** – Create incentive programs that change behaviors towards acceptance and compliance with wellness, well-being and early intervention, including pre-natal, non-smoking, diet, exercise, and safety.	1	2	3	4	5
7	**Minimize Impact of Cost Shifting** – Use consumerism as an alternative to increased cost shifting or higher contributions.	1	2	3	4	5

8	**Implement Optional Consumerism –** Provide new programs and plan options on a voluntary basis.	1	2	3	4	5
9	**Implement Change on a Multi-Year Program –** Establish a HC program with a pre-determined multi-year introduction of options and use of accumulated HRAs and/or options.	1	2	3	4	5
10	**Focus on Information Sharing –** Provide employees with decision support systems and information sources without accounts or incentives or rewards/penalties.	1	2	3	4	5
11	**Use Packaged Programs –** use full integration of plan design, information, disease management, and decision support systems from single vendor.	1	2	3	4	5
12	**Use Existing Vendors –** develop consumerist programs through current vendor relationships only.	1	2	3	4	5
13	**Use "Best of Class" Programs –** use selected vendors that may overlay core benefit designs as long as integration is Non-disruptive and transparent to members	1	2	3	4	5
14	**Move to Private Exchange –** use a private exchange to lower administrative costs and/or offer more employee choice.	1	2	3	4	5
15	**Use Telemedicine/Telehealth –** implement a wide array of new technologies to increase access/convenience to care, offer care options, improve monitoring, and increase compliance.	1	2	3	4	5

Now, having spent a considerable amount of time on the foundational steps to develop a clear understanding and direction for your organization, you are ready for the NEXT STEP – CHANGE. **Video 101**

Chapter 5

The Formula for Change
<u>Video 102</u>

Winston Churchill once said, "You can always count on Americans to do the right thing - after they've tried everything else." Well, the United States has tried many different ways to change healthcare. The goal is to lower the cost, expand access, and improve the quality. We have tried payment reforms, insurance reforms, cost shifting, self-insured funding, HMOs, PPOs, and a myriad of other initiatives. We seem to keep changing or at least trying to change without finding the right solution.

A lot of people talk about and propose change, but how does it actually happen? Is there a process to follow for change? Is there a formula for successful change? Well, I am an actuary – a sort of insurance mathematician – and I like formulas. I found the perfect formula from Paul Ingram PhD, a Kravis Professor of Business at Columbia:

$$D \times V \times P = C$$

The Formula for Change						
Desire	X	Vision	x	Process	=	Change

A. The Desire for Change

The "D" stands for "Desire". The key question to ask is, "Within the organization, is there a desire for something better?" Since many believe individuals and organizations respond more to pain than a promise or desire of something better, the question can be stated in negative terms as "Is the pain/failure of what you are currently doing great enough to require a change?"

The Human Resource department is crucial in stating and reinforcing the organizational desire for change. However, many times the desire for change comes from the CFO or the CEO. But reaching critical mass on the "Desire" for change has its own process. First one must become aware of the possibilities for change. It is critical to identify the organizational pros and cons of any potential change. The next step is to identify the winners and losers resulting from any change. If the initial analysis shows the potential winners are greater or more influential than the potential losers, the stage is set for more detailed research.

After intensive (and usually time consuming) research of products, approaches, and available services a determination is made as to whether all signals indicate a "go or no-go" decision.

The key decisions may involve financial concerns, morale issues, competitive needs, union concerns or other issues unique to the organization. The threshold of moving to the next step is either achieved or not. Without reaching a threshold necessary to support a desire for change, no change is likely to happen. In the above formula, if D=0, then the possibility of C (change) is also zero. The best decision is likely to "put it on the back burner."

The Formula for Change						
No Desire	x	Vision	x	Process	=	**Back Burner**

B. The Vision of Change

The "V" stands for "Vision." A common vision of the future is usually the missing link when attempting sustainable changes. Creating a common vision may start with the HR department, the executive suite, and/or among employees. Without a common vision, an organization is likely to purchase and implement disconnected and potentially contradictory programs and services.

The processes and concepts outlined in this book's subsequent chapters will provide the basis for any organization to develop a successful sustainable HC concept based on a common vision.

In the above formula, if V=0, so C (change) is also zero. Without a common vision and a long term strategy, an organization will likely go through many "expensive and time consuming false starts."

The Formula for Change						
Desire	x	**No Vision**	X	Process	=	**Expensive False Starts**

C. The Process for Change

The "P" stands for "Process." Once there is a desire to change and a common vision is established, the search for the processes of implementation can begin. It is important to find the right vendor(s) or "solution provider(s)" who can match your vision. Do you go with a single integrated solution or seek out "best of class" providers?

The stage of implementing change usually involves a consultant or broker assisting with a "Request for Proposal" or RFP process. In the above formula, if P=0, then C (change) is also zero. If no one can realistically and within budget deliver on the vision, it will halt the process of change and create "frustration" because you cannot find someone who can do what you want to do.

The Formula for Change						
Desire	x	Vision	x	**No Process**	=	**Frustration**

D. Effective Change

Only when all three aspects of change are reached and in alignment with your principles, vision, and strategies will effective sustainable change occur.

The Formula for Change						
Desire	x	Vision	x	Process	=	Change

If your organization has reached the threshold for change and all of the areas – Desire, Vision, and Process – are in alignment, only then can you proceed to a important NEXT STEP – CORPORATE READINESS

> "The secret to change is to focus all of your energy, not on fighting the old but on building the new." – Socrates

Video 102

Chapter 6

Corporate Readiness and Human Capital

If the planning (principles, vision, strategy) leads you to moving forward with "Healthcare Consumerism" there is one more critical step - Corporate Readiness. Corporate Readiness is more than "creating a culture of health" or implementing an "integrated health management" program. In its best form it is a culture of caring and sharing with staff in a sincere way that accepts them as adults worthy of respect.

Before implementing HC, changes may be required across the organization. Other benefits and structures of the organization must be consistent with messages and an emphasis on the concepts of HC that focus on personal responsibility, self-reliance, transparency, and ownership.

Historically employers tried to drive healthcare purchasing behaviors by shifting costs, increasing deductibles, and requiring higher employee premium contributions. Few corporations have taken the time to develop insights into the cost drivers and corporate initiatives needed to support changes in employee behaviors. To be consistent with the concepts of HC, four major areas of employee engagement need to be reviewed throughout the corporation:

1. Shared Rewards - providing employees with something to gain
2. Shared Responsibility – putting employees at risk with something to lose
3. Asset Growth – giving employees something to protect
4. Ownership – allowing employees the freedom to choose

A. Readiness Test for Healthcare Consumerism

The economist Wendy Lynch, PhD has done remarkable work in the area of human capital and healthcare. While at HCMCGroup she developed a scale that measures the level of recognition of Human Capital within an organization. The scale can also be used to determine if implementing HC will likely be successful.

Within each of four areas there are numerous related corporate programs that can show whether your existing corporate environment is compatible with implementing HC.

Award a point for each yes answer, if the answer applies to the *majority* of employees. The maximum score is 20.

Corporate Readiness Test for Healthcare Consumerism	
Shared Rewards (5 Points)	Pts
1 Are employees eligible for a performance bonus?	
2 If employees are eligible for a bonus, do they: a. Know exactly how bonuses will be determined? Or, b. Know that at least part of their bonus is based on individual performance?	
3. Is it possible to earn bonus or profit sharing that is greater than 10% of total salary?	
4 Can employees cash in unused sick leave or paid-time off (PTO) for extra pay?	
5 Survey result "Strongly Agree": *At my company, the people who succeed are those who earn it through their achievement.*	
Shared Responsibility (5 Points)	Pts
1 Do employees have a paid-time-off-bank instead of sick leave?	
2 Are employees compensated less than 100% pay during their Short Term Disability (STD)?	

3	Do most employees have a health plan <u>out-of-pocket</u> maximum of $3000 or higher?	
4	Do most employees have a health plan <u>deductible</u> of more than $1500?	
5	Survey result "Agree": *I protect my health because it is essential to having a successful career*	
Asset Growth (5 Points)		
1	Do you have a 401(k) available with at least a 3% corporate match?	
2	Do you have an HSA or HRA with an annual company deposit of $2000 or more?	
3	Do you have tuition reimbursement for educations?	
4	Is prevention and wellness covered at 100%	
5	Survey result "Very Good/Excellent": *How would you rate your company's emphasis on skill training.*	
Ownership (5 Points)		
1	Do you offer a consumer-driven healthcare or healthcare consumerism plan?	
2	Do employees have access to support for personal financial decisions?	
3	Do employees have access to decision support for health and healthcare decisions?	
4	Are employees encouraged to make independent decisions at work?	
5	Survey results "Agree": *My company asks for input about what benefits are important to workers.*	

On a scale of 1 to 20, if the company scored 1-7 it may not be ready for HC. Other changes within the organization may be needed before or concurrent with implementing of HC.

If the company score was 8-13, the organization has already taken some important steps to support the engagement of employees and will likely find immediate but moderate health plan cost savings.

If the company scored 14 to 20, it is more than ready and will find it is already compatible with a culture of health and respect of employees. It will likely experience optimal results from a well designed program of HC.

Score	Corporate Readiness Test Results
1-7	Make other corporate changes before or concurrent with Health Plan Changes
8-13	Implement for modest impact and cost savings, but develop greater reinforcing consistency across the organization
14-20	Implement for high impact health and healthcare behavioral change and cost savings.

B. Human Capital

Human capital and equipment capital are very different. Unlike machines, employees bring understanding, compassion, mentoring, and flexibility to the job. "Human Capital" includes intelligence, problem solving, creativity, teaming, and an "intrapreneurial" spirit. That is why people or "Human Capital" is the most important asset of any business.

Traditional human capital is purely financial. It is an economic description of an employee's worth or value to a company. It is generally management's view of the value of its hired staff.

The "Health as Human Capital Foundation (HHCF)" defines human capital as a function of three major personal assets offered by each individual:
1. Skill – the education and experiences,
2. Motivation – attitudes and values, and
3. Health – physical and mental capacity.

The impact of human capital, health, and healthcare connects organizational productivity and personal growth. Benefit managers need to better understand this relationship to design and offer benefits that maximize their organizational investment in health and healthcare.

If individuals cannot maintain their health, their economic value to the organization declines. If organizations do not assist and support health for their employees (and family members), they will not receive the optimum productive value from their human capital.

Many employees do not make the connection between maintaining their health and their compensation. Many employers do not connect the impact of the overall work environment to personal responsibility, lifestyle choices, compliance with treatments, and healthy activities of plan members. If personal responsibility is not a part of other aspects of the employees' workplace then expecting optimal engagement by employees in their health is not realistic.

C. "Truly Human Leadership" – Bob Chapman Video

Bob Chapman, CEO Barry-Wehmiller Companies, is a strong proponent of "Truly Human Leadership." It is the degree to which management treats employees as valued intelligent adults. He defines the impact of a Truly Human Leadership as sending staff home at the end of the day – safe, healthy, and fulfilled. The goal is to provide "wellbeing" – a concept much broader than wellness.

Organizations that treat employees with respect and dignity in areas other than health benefits will have lower healthcare costs. Engaging each individual's intellect and creativity as well as personally knowing each and every employee must be a part of the overall business culture. (*e.g.* Does each manager know the names of the spouse and children of each person under their direction?)

This is not a white collar or blue collar distinction. This is not a profit versus not-for-profit distinction. Employees of any skill or education level can be participants in idea generation, product and service improvements, and cost effective changes. Health benefit plans are only a part of the overall environment of engaging employees and supporting good health and healthcare decisions both on and off the job site.

Truly Human Leadership engages employees within and outside of their health plan. Within the health plan it may be health saving accounts and other aspects of HC. It may mean helping employees with financial skills, family issues, or child care. Outside the health plan it includes employees acting and being treated as adults.

It's time to recognize that health and healthcare costs do not stand alone within an organization. Health plan costs cannot be viewed as a single budgetary line item. We now know that the cost of healthcare is not only a function of the individual's health, but the overall culture of an organization.

Most employers know that healthy populations are more productive. Healthy employees will have fewer sick days, increased productivity, improved presenteeism, fewer disabilities, and lower health costs. To create healthy workers, benefits managers have tended to change plan designs, products, and services to better engage employees in plan selection, treatment alternatives, care options, and lifestyle choices.

The development of one's own "personal human capital" creates income opportunities and long term financial growth for individuals. Without health, all the other aspects of personal human capital are quickly diminished. Individual health and a healthy workplace is the link between personal career growth and an organization's productivity interests.

D. Savings Potential – A Composite Case Study

Based on a large data base of employers' information (health costs and corporate culture profiles), the Health as Human Capital Foundation put together an analytical composite of two employers. They analyzed the data to compare apples to apples to show how companies with identical characteristics can have dramatically different healthcare costs.

In the study healthcare costs were "normalized" to show financial results given identical age mix, same gender profile, equal work tenure, same number and types of diagnoses, equal co-morbidities, and the same region of the country.

Company #1 had 84% higher per member healthcare costs ($4,981 versus $2,705) than did Company #2. Surprisingly, the reason is not directly related to healthcare. The difference is how human capital is engaged throughout the organization.

Few corporations have taken the time to develop inclusive ways to engage employees. Surveys and studies have shown that if the first time you expect your employees to act like adults is with their healthcare benefits, you probably will fail in your attempt to get them engaged.

A survey supported by the Institute for Health and Productivity Management found that 62 percent of American businesses and nearly 85 percent of employees say the workplace must play a leadership role in creating a healthier workforce and helping to curb rising healthcare costs. In their own self interest, employees want and need employers to take an active role in creating a healthy workplace.

Bob Chapman Video

Chapter 7

1st Generation
Healthcare Consumerism
Video 107

There are at least five generations of HC that are at differing stages of maturity. We will take each generation and cross reference it with the five building blocks of HC: (1) personal care accounts, (2) health management, (3) condition managements, (4) health literacy, and (5) incentives/rewards. Because the 1st generation is focused on high deductible plan designs, we will first describe (with some duplication to Chapter 2) how both HRAs and HSAs factor into 1st generation HC.

1st Generation HC plans are typically CDHP's sold in response to the June 26, 2002 Treasury ruling that defined Health Reimbursement Arrangements. In the early years there was significant insurer and employer resistance to these plans.

When sold, the early adopters of 1st generation plans allowed them as an option to traditional plans. Minimal co-payment Health Maintenance Organizations (HMOs) had been growing rapidly throughout the 1990's, but cost pressures, high utilization of medical services, and limitations on access to care began to slow their expansion. Employer sponsored group plans were searching for a new approach.

Startup companies Definity and Lumenos successfully challenged the HMOs and traditional insurers by providing cost reducing CDHPs. After years of resistance, large national carriers and Blue-Cross Blue Shield plans began to offer their own high deductible HRA plans in combination with HMO and PPO options. After the 2003 legislation enabled HSA eligible plans, insurers began offering both HRAs and HSAs.

In most cases, employers learned from the limitations of 1st generation plans and moved quickly to later generation concepts and more sophisticated approaches to HC. Below describes 1stgeneration HC plans and each of the key building blocks.

A. Personal Care Accounts

The HC Grid	1st Generation Health & Discretionary Expenses
Personal Care Accounts	Initial Account Only
Wellness & Health Management	100% ACA Mandated Preventive Care
Disease & Condition Management	Information, Health Coach
Decision Support & Health Literacy	Passive Info, Discretionary Expenses, Rx, ER, D-X-L
Incentives & Rewards	Cash, Tickets, Gift Cards, Trinkets,

In 1st generation plans with HRAs an initial employer allocation is made to cover part of the deductible. By regulation, only employers are allowed to make allocations to HRAs. Note that HRAs are "arrangements" rather than "accounts." They are also referred to as "notional accounts" because they are employer promises not actual dollars deposited into a bank account.

HRAs are employer promises of funds that are available to the plan member for healthcare expenses and other allowed HRA uses (Uses are described later in the Chapter on Personal Care Accounts). Employer's can limit, restrict, and/or eliminate the HRA allocations at any time.

With HSA eligible 1st generation plans, both initial employer and employee dollars can be deposited into the account. Once an employer makes an HSA deposit, the dollars are irrevocably owned by the employee.

Employers can decline to make any HSA deposits and only provide the opportunity for employees to deposit tax advantaged dollars into an eligible HSA bank account. If employers offer an HSA eligible plan but do not establish an integrated HSA account, employees can set up their own HSA with a qualified trustee outside the employer sponsored plan. (Details on the option and uses of HSA are described later in the Chapter on Personal Care Accounts)

B. Health Management

The majority of early 1st generation high deductible consumer-driven designs included 100% plan paid preventive care benefits, even before the 2010 Patient Protection and Affordable Care Act (ACA) mandated them. Preventive benefits allow plan participants to focus on maintaining good health and accumulating HRA or HSA funds for future medical needs. With extensive preventive care coverage, there is a greater potential for carry-over of unused funds since the cost of preventive care services will not be deducted from HRA or HSA accounts.

C. Condition Management

Condition management is not a major focus of 1st generation HC. This led to the early criticisms that such plans were only for the young and healthy. 1st generation condition management features include basic healthcare information, access to an online health coach, and call-center support programs focused on specific diseases.

D. Health Literacy / Decisions Support

Health literacy is a developing term that was not used with early 1st generation plans. The original term was "decision support" programs. These included passive web-based information on the cost of discretionary expenses related to prescription drugs, office visits, emergency rooms, and some diagnostic, x-ray, and lab work.

Detailed education and knowledge transfer of health and healthcare information that would engage plan members is limited in most 1ˢᵗ generation plans. In early generation plans, decision support focused on plan selection (if an employer provided options) and primary physician selection within a discounted PPO network of providers.

E. Incentives / Rewards / Penalties

Incentives are financial payments made in advance to encourage participation in an activity. Rewards are financial payments made after successfully meeting an activity goal. Many adopters of HC have found that their populations respond more to penalties than positive encouragements. HC includes both the "carrot" and "stick" approaches. Each organization is different.

1ˢᵗ generation products rarely used additional HRA allocations or HSA deposits for incentives, rewards or penalties. That would come more into play with 2ⁿᵈgeneration consumerism. Instead, typical 1ˢᵗ generation plans provided cash, gift cards, movie tickets, and other trinkets for participation, completion, or meeting the goals of some health related activity.

In total, 1ˢᵗ generation was a great start, but was subject to legitimate criticisms of only being good for the healthy and wealthy. The passage of HSAs at the end of 2003 pushed the market toward better solutions that can meet, if properly designed, the needs of all employees. Market changes have to start somewhere and the successes of 1ˢᵗ generation plans was the foundation for creating a strong demand for 2ⁿᵈ generation plans with a focus on real behavioral change. Further fueling the evolution of HC are new technology developments, personalized incentives, and a proven track record of lowering costs as evidenced by the success of early adopters.

Video 107

48

Chapter 8

2nd Generation
Healthcare Consumerism
Behavioral Change
<u>Video 107</u> *(Same as Chapter 7 video)*

With the passage of HSAs in 2003, most HC plans rapidly evolved into 2nd generation designs with financial incentives that focus on expanded health management, robust condition management services, and health literacy. Most employers implementing 2nd generation programs are seeking to produce measurable results of employee engagement and healthy outcomes.

A. Personal Care Accounts

The HC Grid	2nd Generation Behavioral Changes, Shared Savings
Personal Care Accounts	Activity & Compliance Rewards
Wellness & Health Management	Web-based Behavior Change Support
Disease & Condition Management	Disease Specific Compliance Awards
Decision Support & Health Literacy	Personal Health Mgmt, info with access incentives
Incentives, Rewards, Penalties	Health Incentive Accts, Activity Compliance Incentives

2nd generation HC can support and reward healthy behaviors under different plan designs.

As employers adopt HC strategies, there is a greater need for customized plan and provider selection tools, account monitoring, cost and quality information, and health management support.

HRAs and HSAs are both personal care accounts. However, technically the legal structure of HRAs is an "arrangement" and HSAs are "accounts. HRAs are technically specialized insurance plans containing a promise ("notional account") for funding medical expenses. HSAs are real dollars owned by employees.

The leap to 2nd generation HC is made when organizations change from making an initial HRA allocation or HSA deposit to making additional allocations and deposits during the plan year based on specific plan member actions.

The concept of "Shared Savings" promotes greater participation and compliance with wellness and condition management programs. That is, if employees meet certain cost saving criteria or make plan-recognized healthy choices, funds will be added during the plan year to the HRA or HSA account.

The flexibility of HRAs can support complex 2nd generation wellness and condition management incentive designs. For example: prescription drug copayments, deposits, or withdrawals from the HRA may be predicated on compliance with a disease management program.

Incentive additions to HSAs can also be used if developed within the IRS guidelines. The July 2004 IRS guidelines stated the following:

Question: If under the employer's cafeteria plan, employees who are eligible individuals and who participate in health assessments, disease management programs or wellness programs receive an employer contribution to an HSA, unless the employee elects cash, are the contributions subject to the comparability rules?

IRS Answer: No. The comparability rules under section do not apply to employer contributions to an HSA through a cafeteria plan. In other words, employees must be able to cash out their incentives before they are committed to an HSA.

HRAs and HSAs are not the only ways to reward plan members for engaging in health behaviors. "Pay for Compliance" (P4C) is a term sometimes used for making rewards based upon member behaviors. The multiple versions of P4C are critical to the success of 2nd generation HC. Options include: reduction in cost sharing, lowering member premium contributions, and offering additional benefits.

B. Health Management

Second generation health management programs provide incentives and awards. For example, 2nd generation preventive care plans reward participation for employees taking a wellness assessment (a.k.a. health risk appraisals). In addition, patients who participate in certain predetermined good health activities may receive HRA rewards, points that convert to discounts, rebates, or improved coverage (e.g. non-smoking programs, health club membership, corporate sponsored runs, etc.).

Incentives/rewards have been so successful in increasing participation that approximately two-thirds of the employers who invest in employee wellness use an incentive or reward to drive employee participation. A Quest Diagnostic report showed 60% of employees who participate in wellness programs report that the incentive is a deciding factor in their choice to participate. Bio-metrics (e.g. blood pressure, cholesterol, body mass index, waist size, and A1(c)) are popular for outcome measures that can be used for incentives.

C. Condition Management

Unlike health management programs, employers with 2nd generation condition management programs have lagged behind providing rewards for compliance with medical treatment plans. There has been limited experience and a lack of consensus for determining return on investment (ROI) and the impact of rewards on managing chronic and persistent diseases and conditions.

Some employers and health plans have demonstrated that specific disease management programs improve patient care and reduce complications, but evidence varies widely across health conditions and the types of interventions. The most effective programs for condition management seem to focus on a limited number of conditions and/or the use of health status or health outcomes combined with a focus on information and financial incentives.

D. Health Literacy / Decision Support

Appropriate content, multiple media messaging, and easy to use tools are necessary but not sufficient to change consumer and health behaviors. 2nd generation decision support tools that focus on changing consumer health and healthcare behaviors require active patient involvement with learning, reinforcement, and rewards.

Although measurement of the value of health literacy can be challenging, collection and evaluation of program activity and member feedback is essential. Health literacy is more than annual enrollment help, benefit information, and Summary Plan Descriptions (SPDs).

In 2nd generation plans, health literacy must be an ongoing "CAMPAIGN" that provides support and information throughout the year. It is especially important for organizations to discover the key "learning moments" when plan members are most in need and receptive to information.

E. Incentives / Rewards

With an HRA or HSA that includes incentives, patients can pay for underlying health conditions not covered by traditional insurance.

For example, a patient with high cholesterol and a family history of heart disease might find it valuable to have a CT-heart scan to determine the degree of artery calcification.

Although this test is typically not covered by insurance, the information may help motivate the patient to comply with their anti-cholesterol medication. Similarly, depending on the plan design, consumers who believe in the value of alternative or complementary medicine can potentially use account values based upon their personal care preferences.

These approaches combine personal responsibility with patient financial involvement to encourage program participation and reward compliance. The possibilities are many and depend on what type of behavior an organization is trying to encourage. Incentives, rewards, and/or penalties combined with information that reinforce a culture of health, well-being, self help, and shared responsibility can have a significant beneficial effect on outcomes.

Video 107

Chapter 9

3rd Generation
Healthcare Consumerism
Health & Performance – <u>Video 108</u>

3rd generation HC plans recognize that healthy employees directly impact the corporate bottom line. Companies moving to 3rd generation concepts recognize that health plans are the "maintenance contracts" for their human capital – their most valuable asset. This generation adds a focus on workplace health, safety, and workplace stress management.

A. Personal Care Accounts

The HC Grid	3rd Generation Integrated Health & Performance
Personal Care Accounts	Indiv. & Grp Corporate Metric Rewards
Wellness & Health Management	Worksite Wellness, on-site clinics, safety, Stress & Error reduction
Disease & Condition Management	Population Mgmt, IHM, Integrated Back-to-Work
Decision Support & Health Literacy	Health & Perform. Info, Integrated Health & Work Data
Incentives & Rewards	Non-health corporate metric driven incentives

3rd generation HC focuses the impact on broad business metrics of productivity, absenteeism, impaired presenteeism, turnover, accident rates, turnover, unscheduled sick days, teaming and creativity.

The IRS guidelines give an employer the full power of structuring employee use and applicability of HRAs. 3rd generation HRAs can accommodate incentives and rewards for broader corporate initiatives.

For example, accounts may be increased as a result of individual or groups meeting corporate metrics of operational performance, safety standards, sales, educational standards (e.g. CPE credits), employee of the month, etc. A mixture of individual and group awards adds a new dimension to the total compensation package. With the creative and flexible possibilities of HRAs, they can be the healthcare version of the airlines "frequent flier" program.

HSAs are another great way to accumulate incentives/rewards for health and healthcare decisions that save the employer costs. If plan members are "doing the right things" part of the resulting lower claim costs could be part of a shared savings program. Shared savings reinforces good behaviors. Success breeds success and it sends the message that health and healthcare is a mutually beneficial activity benefiting both the plan sponsor and the member.

Of course, there are ways other than HRAs and HSAs to reward plan members. For example: The cost sharing features (deductibles and copays) can be lowered, employee contributions can be reduced, and new benefit offerings can be added.

B. Health Management

3rd generation health management links individual health to business and operational performance. 3rd generation preventive care emphasizes an array of programs designed to maintain or improve employee functionality and organizational performance. New measurements may need to be established that can make the links among personal safety, occupational hazards, accident prevention, prevention of worksite violence, and stress with overall corporate costs and corporate functionality.

Calculating ROI for prevention and wellness and the direct impact on corporate metrics can be challenging due to the multitude of variables that influence health status and business functionality.

However, some employers are examining the correlation between employee participation in health promotion and wellness programs with direct medical plan costs and some business-unit operational metrics. The trade association H.E.R.O. Health is a leader in such studies. The link between healthcare and other performance issues will continue to develop as third generation plans evolve.

While HIPAA generally prohibits plans from differentiating benefits or premiums based on health status, employers can still design and implement wellness programs with financial incentives. Only a "*bona fide* wellness program" allows for rewards based on a health standard or health outcome (e.g. Body Mass Index, Blood Pressure, Blood nicotine level, cholesterol levels).

To be a "*bona fide* wellness program," the law specifies that the wellness program must meet four requirements:

1. Limit the incentive to a percentage of the cost of coverage (30% under the ACA).
2. Be reasonably designed to promote health or prevent disease.
3. Be available to all similarly situated individuals. There must be a feasible alternative for those that cannot reach the health standard because of a medical condition.
4. Inform employees that individual accommodations and alternatives are available.

It is in an organization's interest to keep employees healthy by implementing prevention and offering wellness-lifestyle or well-being support. It is also important to minimize the claim cost impact of acute episodic conditions with early intervention and wellness-clinical programs. With consumerism, the power of employee self-interest and financial incentives are used to encourage lower costs and better health. Both of which will accrue to the benefit of the organization through lower medical plan claims and increased productivity. New products, start up companies, and creative entrepreneurs are pushing us towards new 3rd-4th-and 5th generation technology solutions.__**Video 119**

C. Condition Management

3rd generation programs focus on impacting not only health and healthcare costs, but corporate metrics, such as: productivity, absenteeism, disability, turnover, unscheduled sick leave, presenteeism, and worker's compensation.

An important tool for discovering the key areas affecting the business entity is to have all employees participate in taking a wellness assessment - also called a Health Risk Appraisal. Aggregate employee survey information and population management tools like wellness assessments can direct an employer's education and worksite assistance efforts. Data supported condition management programs can assist members with better healthcare decisions and favorably impact the organization with healthy employees.

It is difficult to segment 3rd generation condition management programs from other services impacting human capital. The following is a spectrum of programs that when integrated will produce savings for the health benefit budget, but can go further in producing an efficient optimally functional organization. The areas below establish the foundation for a 3rd generation integrated health and performance program.

3rd Generation Integrated Health and Performance		
Plan Design Programs		
Early Intervention	Case Management	Employee Assistance Program (EAP)
Prevention	Disease Management	Absence Management
Wellness	Demand Management	Condition Management
Organizational Support Programs		
Population Management	Culture of Health & Wellbeing	Shared Responsibility
Personal Accountability	Organizational Support	Data Driven Metrics
Quality Management	Shared Savings	Truly Human Leadership

To start, one way to optimize 3rd generation consumerism and health & performance opportunities is to integrate population management with condition management, case management, and quality management.

Strategic Programs	Target Areas	Actions	Program Focus
Population Mgmt	Health & Healthcare Behaviors	Identify Health & Related Costs and Metrics	Diet, Exercise Lifestyle, Stress Management Substance Abuse
Condition Mgmt	Symptoms, Conditions, Functionality, & Improved Performance	Evaluate Personnel & Organizational Opportunities	Identification & Prioritization, Patient Education & Adherence, Provider Support Psycho-social support
Case Mgmt	Patient Assessment, Compliance, & Treatment	Use Data Analytics	Predictive Modeling Personalized support Hi Tech – Hi Touch Support, Co-morbidities
Quality & Cost Mgmt	Incentives, Rewards, & Reimbursements	Integrate with Improving Patient-Provider Relationship	Transparency Tiering on need, cost & quality Vendor Performance Mgmt

D. Health Literacy / Decisions Support

3rd generation health literacy includes more than education on health and healthcare decisions. It includes interactive user-friendly decision support tools. It includes easy to use impactful health and performance metrics for the company.

Aggregated claim and risk assessment data can serve as the foundation to help identify opportunities for ongoing improvement.

Specialized information, assessment, self-help and interventions in areas such as stress though lifestyle and work changes can have a dramatic impact on health & performance issues.

In addition, organizational HR and finance resources can be better leveraged to optimally engage and support the employee's health, well being, and productivity.

For example, the technology of personal wearables can create new avenues of communication, reminder messaging, and reinforcements. There can be an integration of and hot links to HR programs of financial management, leadership training, family support programs, and other corporate self-help and training.

E. Incentives & Rewards

3rd generation incentive programs include rewards for meeting business goals of productivity, absenteeism, turnover, accident rates, etc. Rewards can be based on individual or group metrics.

Creative designs for matching HRA incentives to HSA contributions are possible. For example, employers can match employee HSA contributions with HRA account balances. Of course, the HRA amounts cannot be used for the HDHP deductible coverage, but can be used for the coinsurance (after the deductible) and for non-plan Qualified Medical Expenses (QMEs).

HSAs could be positioned as employee contributions and HRAs as employer contributions. With this the employee gains the maximum tax advantage and portability of HSAs and the employer maintains the flexibility and cash flow advantages of HRAs.

By using the HRA matching approach for HSAs an employer can continue to develop reward programs that directly affect the corporate metrics targeted.

Video 108	**Video 119**

Chapter 10

3rd Generation
Healthcare Consumerism & Stress Management
Video 115

A major part of the 3rd generation of HC is related to stress and depression in the workplace. Stress and depression costs (including co-morbid costs) for U.S. businesses are over $200 billion per year according to a 2015 study by the Journal of Clinical Psychiatry. 3rd generation programs of stress management can link healthcare, consumerism, and organizational quality, safety, and error reduction programs.

Improved product quality and productivity can result with focused efforts to address areas such as stress and depression in the workplace.

One thing is certain – if an organization does not have a structured stress management program for employees, it is 100% certain that employees will deal with their stress in other ways (e.g. comfort food, alcohol, drugs, smoking, etc.)

U. S. Surgeon General David Satcher once said, "There is no health without mental health." Similarly, there is no effective program of HC without mental healthcare consumerism. It is a basic requirement for any employer implementing HC plans to deal with stress, depression, and more serious mental illnesses. It is important for employers to understand the clinical and cost inter-relationships between "mind care" and "body care."

Studies show that stress impacts an organization in many ways:

1. Health care - 21.5% of total health care costs
2. Turnover - 40% of the primary reasons that employees leave a company
3. Impaired Presenteeism - 50% of impaired presenteeism is a function of stress
4. Disability - 33% of all disability and workers' compensation costs
5. Unscheduled Sickness - 50% of the primary reasons that employees take unscheduled absence days

To work for everyone, HC must help the sickest and most vulnerable. Mental illnesses present a unique challenge. Depression is a sickness where patients tend to push away care givers. Many with depression and co-existing physical illnesses will deny their need for care, ignore treatment advice, skip appointments, and are highly non-compliant with medications.

A 2014 Kaiser poll showed 48% of employers offer wellness in the workplace. But, a 2013 survey by the American Psychological Association's Center for Organizational Excellence found that despite growing awareness of the importance of a healthy workplace, fewer than half of employees said their organizations provide sufficient resources to help them manage stress (36 percent) and meet their mental health needs (44 percent).

Stress has a distinct correlation with medical issues in other body systems. Stress Directions, a leading consultancy on stress, found: "44% of all adults suffer adverse health effects from stress; 75 to 90% of all physician office visits are for stress-related ailments and complaints; stress is linked to the 6 leading causes of death - heart disease, cancer, lung ailments, accidents, cirrhosis of the liver, and suicide."

Stress Directions, Inc. outlines the following relationships:

Related & Embedded Healthcare Costs from Stress	
Source of Stress	Major Body System Affected by Stress
Job	Muscular System
Family	Digestive System
Personal	Cardiovascular
Social	Emotional
Financial	Endocrine, Immune
Environmental	Cognitive

If your plan is not properly dealing with member stress, you will increase the cost of treating the manifestations of stress in those body systems where health costs are covered. These correlations are why well-being is a growing area of interest. Providing support programs for the whole person whether at work or at home will lower health costs and improve productivity.

The Occupational Safety and Health Administration (OSHA) has declared stress a "hazard of the workplace." There are at least three separate, but related costs of stress in the workplace:

1. **Direct Mental Health Costs** – as separate diagnoses these costs can range from low to high costs.
2. **Co-Morbid Condition Costs** – many times the more obvious physical health symptoms are treated, but the underlying mental health issue is ignored.
3. **Indirect Corporate Costs** – these are costs from absenteeism, disability, unscheduled sick days, loss of teaming, relationship conflicts, etc.

With the assistance of many national mental health experts and organizations, Healthcare Visions, Inc. has organized a chart showing the relationships among the three types of corporate costs.

Organizational Costs of Stress and Emotional Conditions				
Medical Intensity	Type of Condition	"Direct" Mental Health Costs	Co-Morbid Condition Costs	"Indirect" Corporate Costs
Low Cost	Frustration Anxiety Low Stress Minor Depression	Low	Tobacco Use Sleeplessness Colds/Flu Blood Pressure	**Moderate–High** Increased Errors Presenteeism Loss of Teaming
Medium Cost	Moderate Stress Depression Anger Attention Deficit Disorder PTSD	Medium Cost	Hypertension Musculoskeletal Digestive Gastrointestinal	**Moderate-High** Unsch Absences Poor Morale Relation Conflicts Lost Productivity
High Cost	High Stress Major Depression Schizophrenia Bipolar Disorder Obsess Compulsive Panic Disorder Anorexia-Bulimia	High	Cardiovascular Cancer Diabetes Asthma Back Pain Alcoholism	**High** Low Productivity Divorce Turnover Early Retirement Worker's Comp Disability
Extreme	Violence Suicide	High	Accidents Burns	**High** Death Work Violence Disaster Recovery

Companies can no longer treat stress, depression, or any mental illness as a single diagnosis. Because of coexisting mental illnesses, many employees will not effectively recover from or stabilize chronic and persistent conditions such as diabetes, asthma, heart conditions, hypertension, or cancer unless an effective stress management program is implemented.

A 2005 study for Dupont Company by the University of Pennsylvania showed that depression, when measured by its impact on total costs (direct and indirect costs), was the highest corporate cost medical condition. The second highest total cost was from musculoskeletal issues that likely also involved stress related costs.

Medical, clinical, and medication therapies have advanced such that clinical depression and other mental health conditions have cure rates equal to and greater than many medical conditions. Clinical depression can be cured. Treatments work. Medications are effective. No company, large or small, can avoid the costs of depression. Divorce, disability, and violence in the workplace can hit anyone at anytime. According to the Institute of Medicine 30,000 people die each year from suicide, and 90% had diagnosable and treatable depression. For a small employer the results can be devastating if a key employee or executive suffers from clinical depression.

Tom Johnson, former CEO of CNN News, likes to say, *"If a company's computers crashed and corporate production ground to a halt, the CEO would demand immediate action to re-establish the "corporate brains." In developing a "knowledge-based" workforce, it is just as important for CEOs to take care of mental health and the "central computer" – the brain - within each employee."*

Most employers do not understand the complexities of clinical mental health diagnoses. They do not know what it means to have schizophrenia, a somatoform disorder, a factitious disorder, or get a multi-axial assessment. Tom Johnson understood as he often suffered from serious bouts of clinical depression. Tom has dedicated his life to helping others deal with the debilitating effects of depression.

Video 115

Case Study

As an actuary and mathematician, I was trained in numbers and actuarial science. Many of you may also be analysts, doctors, lawyers, CEOs, economists, or researchers. Let's throw away the numbers for a moment and look at the lives of real people.

Let me tell you about a young man, age 30, who suffered multiple inherited physical problems: a blood disorder, clotting concerns, pulmonary hypertension, and other unfathomable sources of pain and suffering. Combined with depression and the stigma of an emotional disorder, this young man was frequently non-compliant with care and treatment. Unlike other physical illnesses, depression typically causes the patient to avoid care. He pushed away the very help that was needed. He pushed away family support and friends that cared.

No young strapping 6'5" 260 pound young man wants his forehead stamped with the stigma of mental illness. He was not going to be classified as "crazy", see a "shrink", or go to a "nut house" for care. No, he was a high school basketball star with the athletic promise most boys just dream about. In his mind, he didn't need care, he was who he was. He didn't accept or understand chemical imbalances. In his mind, "Real men are strong enough."

In 2005 the years of depression and physical decline took its toll. The death certificate read pulmonary hypertension. But, I can tell you the real cause was stigma and major depression that prevented this young adult from seeking or accepting the medical and life saving care that he needed.

Chris Golden was my step-son. His mother and I buried Chris on May 5, 2005. Look at all the ROI numbers, but never forget. This is not about numbers. It's about people and saving lives. It's about the Chris Golden's of the world.

Chapter 11

4th Generation
Healthcare Consumerism
Personalized Healthcare – <u>Video 109</u>

There are many advanced aspects of 4th generation HC already being implemented. However, 4th generation HC concepts are a collection of developing and likely future programs where some may require legal, regulatory, and/or technology changes before becoming real. Planning for the future and being strategically consistent with the prospects of 4th generation concepts will prove valuable for any plan.

A. Personal Care Accounts

The HC Grid	4th Generation Personalized Care
Personal Care Accounts	Specialized Accts, Matching HRAs, Expanded QMEs
Wellness & Health Management	Genomics, Predictive Modelling, Push Technology
Disease & Condition Management	Wire-less cyber support, Cultural DM, Holistic Care
Decision Support & Health Literacy	Arrive in time information, information therapy, targeted messaging
Incentives & Rewards	Personal Develop. Plan Incentives, Health Status Related

4th generation personal care accounts focus on the individual characteristics of each member and their related lifestyle needs.

In a 4th generation HC world with legislative changes, personal care accounts may morph or evolve into universal accounts that include the flexibility of HRAs and the portability of HSAs.

As a part of the Cures Act, "HRA Only" financing was passed on December 7, 2016 and signed into law on December 13, 2016 with an effective date of January 1, 2017 (plan years beginning after December 31, 2016).

The Cures Act focuses mainly on speeding up drug approvals through the Food and Drug Administration, but an important additional feature of the law created a new type of HRA called a "Qualified Small Employer Health Reimbursement Arrangement" (QSEHRA).

The Cures Act overturns a previous ruling by the Internal Revenue Service that precluded employers from using a defined contribution "HRA only" approach to subsidize their employees' purchase of individual plans. This new law allows employers with fewer than 50 employees to fund out-of-pocket medical expenses and/or subsidize premiums for the purchase of individual health plans with tax advantage QSEHRAs. To qualify:

1. Employer must be fewer than 50 employees and full-time equivalents, and
2. Don't sponsor a group health plan.

The requirements placed on the QSEHRA are:

1. Employer only funding (cannot do any salary reduction)
2. Maximum annual amounts are $4,950 for single coverage, and $10,000 for family coverage.
3. QSEHRA maximums are adjusted annually for inflation
4. Must be offered to all full-time employees, except:
   a. Those not yet completed the 90 day waiting period,
   b. Are under age 25,
   c. Who are covered by a collective bargaining agreement, or
   d. Part-time seasonal employees.
5. Notice of QSEHRA must be provided at least 90 days in advance.

If the requirements of the QSEHRA are not met, the use of traditional HRAs are still disallowed under the ACA unless there is an attached ACA qualified health plan.

HRAs and HSAs can be used for QMEs covered under section 213(d) of the IRS tax code. The IRS defines and can expand QME's by regulations. New QMEs can be added as medical practices and public interests change. For example, in the future the IRS may have pressure to expand the definition of QME to include cosmetic surgery and other personal care services. There are currently strong arguments that cosmetic surgery is needed to improve the psychological and physical needs for health and wellbeing.

HSAs are ideal for ownership and true portability. The immediate 100% vesting of HSAs and the ability of both employees and employers to contribute to HSAs is a great advantage in establishing ownership and the potential for sizeable accumulations. Even outside third parties (e.g. family, charities) can contribute to one's HSA.

Employers may want to allow employees to add to their HSAs with credits from unused vacation or sick leave. Both HRAs and HSAs need to accommodate personal lifestyle expenses such as, alternative medicines and acupuncture. Employees will want the ability to use debit/credit cards to cover internet medical purchases and cyber-office visits.

In 4th generation HC, the issues that will grow in importance are security and portability of HRA accounts. Legislation will be required to create individual HRAs for true portability. Employees will want continued access to fund accounts post-employment. In addition, vesting issues will be important to employees to secure the value of the accounts. When compared to HSAs, employees may ultimately expect "notional interest" on HRAs. If not initially allowed by the employer, demand will grow for more immediate use of the funds for non-plan QMEs and use of HSAs for paying health premiums.

B. Health Management

4th generation health management focuses on personalized health and healthcare needs. Personalized care utilizes member genomics, proteomics, predictive modelling, and push technology. Preventive care includes both lifestyle changes and clinical treatments.

Connected to various services through the Internet of Things (IoTs), cyber-monitors will provide real time feedback on health status, lifestyle, and health metrics. There is already a "diabetes cell phone" that has a testing attachment, transmits blood sugar levels, and will call with reminders if the tests are not transmitted. Healthcare cyber-feedback will provide daily results of calorie intake versus expenditures and suggest a dietary menu for upcoming meals.

Much like Travelocity can monitor airlines for flight specials, a potential service could be a cyberhealth-aide that will monitor websites for health specials (*e.g.* spa vacations, exercise equipment, medication discounts). A personalized cyber-aide may seek out and suggest health related vacation packages or personalized exercise equipment through internet searches or automatic cyber-auctions.

C. Condition Management

4th generation condition management includes culturally sensitive disease management, measures individual outcomes, and supports personal health status. For example, culturally sensitive disease management would reflect how differently cultures view weight and BMI. By its very nature, 4th generation personalized care is not a one-size-fits-all program.

4th generation condition management programs will focus on compliance and monitoring of mental and physical concerns. Patients with heart conditions, diabetes, COPD, and asthma will find life saving alerts and rapid provider responses to changes in vital signs. Patients with apnea will have sleep patterns and disruptions monitored. The efficacy of equipment and treatment plans will be tuned to personal needs.

D. Health Literacy / Decisions Support – <u>Video 116</u>

As 4th generation health literacy concepts develop, solution providers are likely to provide "arrive in time" information and services at critical moments for care. The 4th generation expands health literacy to include personalized "information therapies" that are consistent and compatible with specific provider "clinical therapies."

"Information therapy" is the prescription of specific, evidence-based medical information to a patient, caregiver, or consumer at just the right time to help that person make a specific health decision or behavior change. It is the ultimate consumer decision support aid.

For example, (per Healthwise) prescribing "information therapy" for each of the following tests and treatments can provide the basis for a support service of great value to both the plan and its members:

1. Prostate surgery
2. Back surgery
3. ACL surgery
4. Coronary artery bypass surgery
5. Medication for depression
6. End-of-life care
7. Prescription of beta-blockers following heart attacks
8. Early-stage breast cancer testing
9. Colon cancer screenings
10. Immunizations and eye test reminders for diabetics

4th generation decision support tools will focus on the individual needs of each member. "Information therapy" as promoted by Healthwise is a term that suggests the active use of patient oriented information with clinical outcomes based medicine. Information needs to be embedded into the process of care—as information therapy.

Some aspects of personalized healthcare are already developing. The future will include mind-boggling decision support systems and wireless connections that link each person to a personalized health and healthcare cyber-support system. Imagine a world with a cyber-aide that continuously searches the internet with a personal profile of health and healthcare needs. Such cyber-support systems can be built to profile activity and anticipate areas of interest.

With good information consumers will be better equipped to fully accept their role in the new world of consumerism.

E. Incentives / Rewards

4th generation incentives and rewards will be designed to meet individual needs and personal health and healthcare targets. 4th generation HC will focus on individual health status and individual outcomes from goals achieved. Personalized health metrics can be set to meet individualized health status incentives. In cases where health metrics are not possible, personalized non-health goals can be set to allow plan members to receive program incentives.

Video 109

Video 116

Chapter 12

5th Generation
Healthcare Consumerism
Community Health – <u>Video 111</u>

Like the Spanish explorer Juan Ponce de Leon, we have all wished for an eternal fountain of youth. Today's medical miracles seem to treat death like a disease to be cured. In reality the best we can hope for is a long productive life. Healthcare Consumerism is the path for "Patient-Centered" care that starts with personal responsibility and leads us from today's concerns about health and healthcare to a fulfilling life with productive longevity.

5th generation HC is called Community Health. It is about socially engaging community, family support, friends, and social media to support a meaningful connected healthy lifestyle. Social networking is growing as a driving force in many parts of our lives. A PricewaterhouseCoopers study found that nearly a third (32%) of consumers have used some form of social media for healthcare purposes. The self-absorbed Baby-boomer "Me" generation is giving way to technologies of GenerationX and the sharing communities of the Millennials on Facebook, Instagram, Snapchat, Twitter, Linked-In, Plaxo, and YouTube.

Important insights to the future and 5th generation HC comes from a book called *"Blue Zones"* by Dan Buettner (https://www.bluezones.com/). In Blue Zones he studied cultures around the world where people are living longer (high percentage older than age 100) and enjoying more productive lives (by 10 years or more). By relating the Blue Zone findings to the evolution of HC, we can see a 5[th]generation that differs from the first four by moving consumerism from:

1. Personalized (self)………. to Community (others)
2. Health…………………… to Productive Longevity
3. Self-help………………… to Helping Others

4. Being Served .... to Sharing
5. Taking .... to Giving
6. Secular .... to Spiritual
7. Monetary .... to Emotional
8. Head (logic) .... to Heart (feelings)

A. Personal Care Accounts

The HC Grid	5th Generation Community Health & Productive Longevity
Personal Care Accounts	Volunteer Vessels, Pay Forward, Charitable Giving
Wellness & Health Management	Natural Resource Flows, Longevity more than Health
Disease & Condition Management	Functionality, Community, Faith & Spirituality
Decision Support & Health Literacy	Friendship Pods, Wisemen, Sharing Circles, Social networks
Incentives & Rewards	Psychic Rewards, Recognition, Honor, Respect, Love

A 5th generation world shifts from financial incentives to intrinsic emotional incentives and charitable rewards.

We all know from psychology 101 and Maslow's hierarchy that changing behaviors with financial incentives has diminishing returns.

Unlike HSAs or HRAs, 5th generation personal care accounts will not be about accumulating money for self. They will include accumulating funds or credits for charitable giving, "paying it forward" accounts, and recognition of volunteer giving.

B. Health Management

The goal of wellness or health management programs will no longer be getting healthy, but will focus on having a long and productive life. For employers, it may mean increasing support for walking teams, group activities, worksite yoga, and group meditation. Corporate health events will include family and friends, not just employees. To promote teaming and group support, corporate health clubs will be open to dependents, friends, and neighbors.

Health treatments will recognize the interaction between mind and body. Stress measurements will become as critical as physical biometric testing. Commonly used depression screening instruments include the Patient Health Questionnaire (PHQ) in various forms and the Hospital Anxiety and Depression Scales in adults, the Geriatric Depression Scale in older adults, and the Edinburgh Postnatal Depression Scale (EPDS) in postpartum and pregnant women.

C. Condition Management

New brain science discoveries will support psycho-physical initiatives in wellness and condition management programs. For disease or condition management programs, the emphasis will shift from recovery to functionality. It will no longer be acceptable to simply eliminate symptoms or use traditional medical treatments to deal with chronic conditions.

The ultimate measurement will be functionality. The World Health Organization's (WHO) International Classification of Functioning, Disability, and Health (ICF) will become a more commonly used measurement and diagnostic tool. Effective treatments will include 4th generation tools of genomic testing and interventions, predictive modeling, and proteomics. The goal will be for individuals to return to doing their jobs effectively, adequately perform the activities of daily living, continue social contacts, and participate in desired lifestyle activities. Health plans will encourage the development of disease specific teams and support groups working towards common health goals.

Key personal relationships will develop as "friendship pods." 5th generation HC plans will formulate, connect and encourage mentoring and "Wisemen" counsels to help others in need. Methodist structures similar to its "Steven Ministry" will create neighbor to neighbor health support and palliative listening leaders.

Spiritual support will be available through worksite programs similar to Marketplace Ministries (http://www.marketplaceministries.com/). Website connections similar to Caring Bridge (https://www.caringbridge.org/) will allow family and friends to assist others in need of medical and life needs during critical health events.

D. Health Literacy / Decision Support

Information and decision support programs will expand to include concepts such as "sharing circles" and "mentoring groups." "Cyber-health aides" will use push technology to expand and link information therapies with clinical therapies. We will learn both from those who have experience and those creative individuals who are experimenting with new ideas.

Clinical and lifestyle information will be shared across generations. Physicians and other providers of care will be supplemented not just with paraprofessionals, but with life coaches. Practical lifestyle insights will be shared from an informed experienced trusted circle of personal advisers and mentors.

E. Rewards / Incentives

Incentives will shift from financial to psychic rewards of recognition, honor, respect and love for others. Faith, hope and spirituality will become an important feature of recovery, functional improvement programs, incentives, and support. Believing in something bigger than one's self can have strong healing and behavioral impacts.

Regardless of one's personal health, assisting, helping, or teaching someone less fortunate is a powerful psychic positive.

In general, the theme of the 5th generation HC will be "Learn, Connect, and Share." 5th generation HC provides collaboration with others. It taps into ideas, wisdom, experiences, and knowledge of what works and what doesn't, including lifestyle support and help in selecting solution providers. It is about serving others, not just helping yourself.

A 5th generation mindset is less individually competitive and materialistic. 5th generation participants want to be engaged in meaningful work but enjoy life, family, and contribute to the community. For older individuals it is about moving from career success to community significance. There will be more volunteering, giving, sharing of wisdom, and support to others.

Video 111

Chapter 13

Personal Care Accounts
The Promise of Demand Control
Video 112 (Same as Chapter 2)

Personal care accounts have become the core feature of HC. Any plan design can have an HRA and/or an FSA personal spending account attached to it. HSAs require a legally defined High Deductible Health Plan. The key to behavioral change under consumerism is the ability to reward and incentivize members for good behaviors. In particular, HRAs and HSA eligible plans can be used to motivate change with initial personal care account balances and subsequent incentive reward additions. Below shows the growth in the percentage of companies offering such plans.

Surveys below are from different sources and measure different populations (sizes and regions may vary within each survey from year to year). Clearly, larger employers are paving the way and demonstrating the value of personal care accounts. The information is shown to indicate the strong growth and acceptance of personal care accounts.

The Growth of Account-based Plans (HSAs & HRAs)					
% of Companies with Health Benefits Offering Account-Based Plans by Year					
Year	**Kaiser** (All Sizes)	**PwC**	**Mercer** (10+Ee's)	**Mercer** (500+Ee's)	**UBA**
2016	28%	32%	25%	76% (proj)	25.7%
2015	26%	31%	29%	59%	25.2%
2014	27%	26%	27%	48%	24.3%
2013	23%	21%	23%	39%	24.1%
2012	31%	17%	22%	36%	22.5%
Sources: Kaiser Family Foundation-Employee Health Benefits, Annual Surveys					
PwC Health and Well-being Touchstone Surveys					
Mercer's National Survey of Employer-Sponsored Health Plans					
United Benefit Advisors Health Plan Surveys					

HSAs are more popular with employer-based health plans than are HRAs.

Growth of HRA and HSA Separately				
% of Companies with Health Benefits Offering Either HRA & HSA Eligible Plans by Year				
HSA Eligible Plans				
Year	All Sizes	Fewer than 1000 Employees	1000-4999 Employees	5000+ Employees
2016	63%	52%	69%	69%
2015	56%	48%	58%	70%
2014	47%	39%	52%	59%
2013	39%	35%	40%	46%
Plans with HRA				
Year	All Sizes	Fewer than 1000 Employees	1000-4999 Employees	5000+ Employees
2016	17%	15%	14%	24%
2015	18%	14%	20%	23%
2014	15%	11%	15%	25%
2013	20%	18%	20%	25%
Sources: PwC Health and Well-being Touchstone Surveys				

Regional Growth of Account-Based Plans					
% of Companies with Health Benefits Offering Account-Based Plans By Region and Year					
Year	North East	South East	North Central	Central	West
2016	34.4%	32.5%	26.6%	21.0%	14.2%
2015	29.2%	22.9%	22.5%		
2014	26.2%	18.5%	29.4%	21.9%	7.8%
2013	24.1%	15.1%	22.6%	17.6%	6.9%
2012	12.1%	12.4%	2.5%	4.0%	0.7%
2011	18.1%	16.5%	9.9%	5.8%	13.1%
2010	6.9%	7.2%	1.4%	0.7%	2.3%
Sources: United Benefit Advisors Health Plan Surveys					

Growth in HSA Account Balances			
Total Consumer HSA Account Balances (in Billions)			
Year	Carry-over Balances	Net New Deposits	Total Account Balances
2016 (est)	$31.0 B	$5.4 B	$36.4 B
2015	$26.0 B	$4.2 B	$30.2 B
2014	$21.0 B	$3.2 B	$24.2 B
2013	$17.1 B	$2.3 B	$19.3 B
2012	$13.7 B	$1.7 B	$15.5 B
2011	$11.1 B	$1.1 B	$12.2 B
2010	$9.0 B	$0.9 B	$9.9 B
Source: Devenir HSA Market Survey and Research Report			

Once the plan design(s) framework is selected by an employer, the type, structure, flexibility, and use of personal care accounts can be matched with the benefit strategy. Each type of account (FSA, HRA, and HSA) has different rules and legal requirements.

Employers will need to consider the multiple plan design options and effectively integrate selected personal care account(s) with the complexity of advanced HC including limited use accounts, deposit amounts, rewards incentives, investment options, withdrawal rules, penalties, etc.

There are important differences in HRAs and HSAs and their use in a multi-generational strategy. HSAs are very desirable because both plan members and employers (and even third parties) can contribute with triple tax advantages. Because there is no required plan design, HRAs may offer the best solution for a creative and flexible shared-savings plan design. The best of all worlds would be a combination account with the flexibility of HRAs and the portability of fully vested HSAs.

Differences in HRAs and HSA Personal Care Accounts for Supporting Behavioral Change Generations 1, 2, & 3			
Personal Care Account	**Generation 1** Initial Account Only	**Generation 2** Activity & Compliance Rewards	**Generation 3** Individual & Group Rewards
Health Reimbursement Arrangement	Employer only Contrib. Cannot be cashed out Healthcare use only Substantiated Records Any Initial Amount Notional Acct.	Generation 1 Plus Activity & Compliance Rewards	Generation 1 Plus Activity & Compliance Rewards Flexible Individual & Group Rewards
Health Savings Account	Amounts Limited by Law 100%Vested/Portable Real Dollars Employer & Employee Contributions Must cash option All receive same amount or same % of deductible Can be used (with 20% penalty) for non-health expenses Non-Substantiated Records	Generation 1 Plus Activity & Compliance Rewards	Generation 1 Plus Activity & Compliance Rewards Difficult to use for group incentives

Differences in HRAs and HSA Personal Care Accounts for Supporting Behavioral Change Generations 4 & 5		
Personal Care Account	**Generation 4** Personalized & Specialized	**Generation 5** Community Sharing
Health Reimbursement Arrangement	Generation 1 Plus Personalized Notional Accounts Specialized Notional Accounts Matching HSAs & HRAs Employer sets rules for termination Potential expansion of QMEs by IRS	Generation 1 Plus Volunteer "Vessel" Accounts Replace with Intrinsic Psychic Rewards
Health Savings Account	Generation 1 Plus Activity & Compliance Rewards Can use matching HRAs Potential expansion of QMEs by IRS	Generation 1 Plus Activity & Compliance Rewards Volunteer "Vessel" Accounts Pay forward use of HSAs Charitable Giving Replace with Intrinsic Psychic Rewards

A. Flexible Spending Accounts (FSAs)

The first tax-advantaged personal care account was the FSA. Established in 1979 under Section 125 of the Internal Revenue Code, monies put into an FSA by either an employer or employee are excludible from income, must be used for qualified medical expenses, and operate under an annual use-it-or-lose-it requirement. This use-it-or-lose-it feature requires that employees project the amount of money that they will spend that will not otherwise be reimbursed by their health plans (e.g. deductible, coinsurance, non-plan QMEs).

FSAs are attractive tax advantaged accounts for employees who anticipate and project either significant or predetermined medical expenses in a given year. The FSA contribution is set and fixed at the beginning of the year. The major disadvantage is that only a portion ($500) of unused funds can be carried over from one plan year to the next. The inability to carry over all unused FSAs, causes economic distortions as members tend to increase utilization on unnecessary and unneeded supplies and services as the year draws to a close and any remaining FSA dollars are at risk of forfeiture.

B. Health Reimbursement Arrangements

HRAs allow for carry-over of unused amounts. The 2002 IRS guidance confirmed that as long as HRAs meet certain requirements, they can be offered in connection with nearly any type of employer health plan to pay for medical benefits on a tax-free basis. One of the key options of HC is using the flexibility of HRAs, allowing them to be used in several ways to achieve employers' benefit and behavioral change objectives.

1. First, HRAs can be used to pay for plan deductibles, coinsurance, and copayments. That is, HRAs can be used to pay for plan defined covered expenses otherwise paid by the employee with after tax dollars. The processing and recognition of HRA payments would go through the normal plan payment adjudication.

2. Second, employers can establish whether or not HRAs can be used for non-plan covered expenses that the IRS recognizes as "qualified medical expenses" (QMEs) under IRC section 213(d). The processing of these payments can be provided by several entities, an insurance carrier, a third party administrator (TPA), BCBS plans, and specialty processors.

Traditionally, there has been a requirement for paper handling, review, and certification of submitted expenses as meeting the 213(d) standards. The IRS has approved the use of electronic processing of claims with certain safeguards to assure they are qualified medical expenses. This IRS approval of electronic processing allows for cost effective "debit/credit" card use to draw on FSA, HRA, and HSAs.

3. The third way (if established by the employer) of using HRA funds is to pay for health insurance premiums. For example, HRAs can be used to pay for COBRA, Retiree Medical, Long Term Care, and other medical insurance plans.

The IRS guidelines give the employer the full power of structuring the employee use, access, and the applicability of HRA funds. Multiple uses can be phased in over a period of years. For example, an employer may initially restrict HRA funds to deductibles and other cost sharing features of the medical plan. In subsequent years or for amounts in excess of some dollar level, an employer may allow extended use of HRAs for non-plan QMEs. Introduction of HC should consider a pre-planned and announced multi-year strategy.

The 2002 IRS guidance clarified that appropriately structured HRAs are not subject to the following restrictions otherwise applicable to FSAs:

- The prohibition against a benefit that defers compensation by permitting employees to carry over unused elective contributions or plan benefits from one plan year to another plan year;
- The requirement that the maximum amount of reimbursement must be available at all times during the coverage period;
- The mandatory twelve-month period of coverage;
- The limitation that medical expenses reimbursed must be incurred during the period of coverage.

C. HRA Only

HRAs are technically insurance plans. Pre-ACA stand-alone HRAs were allowed and used, especially by small employers. An ACA ruling then prohibited stand-alone HRAs as they did not meet the ACA requirements for insurance plans (e.g. unlimited lifetime maximums, essential benefits).

However, on December 13, 2016 the Cures Act was signed into law that reinstated the stand-alone HRA effective January 1, 2017 for groups of fewer than 50. Employers can use a stand-alone HRA to fund health expenses and/or provide support for the purchase of individual policies. This allows small employers to return to a "defined contribution" that can fix their cost to a specific dollar subsidy.

C. The Ordering of HRAs and FSAs

Generally, under regulations governing FSAs, a medical expense may not be reimbursed from a medical FSA, if the expense is reimbursable under any other part of the medical plan or by any other health plan. Under normal IRS rules, if coverage is provided under both an HRA and an FSA for the same medical expense, the HRA amounts must be exhausted before reimbursements are permitted under the FSA. However, in the 2002 IRS ruling they allowed reversal of the ordering. A violation does not occur if medical plan has contract language that is properly written. A plan with a combination of accounts cannot allow for double reimbursements.

D. Health Savings Accounts (HSAs)

Effective January 1, 2004, Federal legislation created HSAs. HSAs can be funded by employers or employees and they are portable. HSAs are tax-free income to employees, they accumulate tax-free, and they are not taxed when withdrawn for eligible medical expenses.

Contributions to an HSA are deductible in determining adjusted gross income (AGI). Employer contributions to an HSA (including salary reduction contributions in cafeteria plans) are excludable from gross income and wages for employment tax purposes to the extent the contribution would be deductible if made by the employee. For policyholders and covered spouses age 55 or older, additional "catch up" contributions of $1000 per year are allowed and specified in the law so that the HSA annual contribution limit is greater than the otherwise applicable limits.

Generally, an HSA eligible plan cannot provide benefits before the deductible is satisfied, but there is an exception for preventive care benefits. Originally the IRS guidance provided a safe harbor list of preventive benefits. With the passage of the ACA the definitions of preventive care benefits was made consistent with the 100% mandated preventive care benefits in the ACA. Generally these include – annual physicals, immunizations and screening services, as well as routine prenatal and well-child care, tobacco cessation programs and obesity weight-loss programs. Preventive care generally does not include treatment of existing conditions.

The IRS has also made it clear prescription drug benefits cannot be provided before the deductible of the HSA eligible plan has been satisfied.

F. Qualified Medical Expenses – Substantiation and Coverage

The IRS requires third party substantiation of HRA and FSA reimbursements as legitimate qualified medical expenses (QME) under Section 213(d). IRS guidelines released in December 2003 **do not** require third party substantiation for HSAs. However, if a member wants to have HSA reimbursements count towards the HDHP deductible the claims must be submitted for plan coverage adjudication.

Generally, HSAs, FSAs and HRAs can be used to reimburse IRS defined QMEs under Section 213(d) of the IRS Code. In 2003, Revenue Ruling 2003-12 expanded the definition of QME to include certain over-the-counter drugs (OTC). Later, HHS ruled that OTC drugs would need to be certified by a physician to qualify for reimbursements (in essence creating a prescription for a non-prescription medication). With some complications, the rulings allow reimbursement for OTC drugs that are used to alleviate or treat personal sickness or injury of the employee or the employee's spouse or dependents but disallows reimbursement for purchases of items that are "merely beneficial to the general health" of the employee (or spouse or dependents).

For plan members with claims less than the HDHP deductible level in a given year, the difference in substantiation rules is a significant simplification for HSAs over FSAs and HRAs. The HSA ruling parallels a previous ruling on Medical Savings Accounts (MSA) – a precursor to HSAs that was passed in 1997 on a limited test basis.

Congress intended HSAs to follow many of the general guidelines set for MSAs. Non-substantiation opened the door for banks and other institutions to act as HSA trustees and offer HSAs directly to the public.

Video 112

Chapter 14

Specialty Use Personal Care Accounts

It can be complicated but valuable for an organization to consider various combinations and uses of personal care accounts. Below are legal but rarely used specialty designs.

A. Limited Purpose HRAs and FSAs

A limited-purpose Health FSA pays or reimburses benefits for "permitted coverages" (but not for insurance or for long-term care services).

A limited-purpose HRA pays or reimburses benefits for "permitted insurance." That is, for a specific disease or illness policy or a plan that provides a fixed amount per day (or other period) for hospitalization or other "permitted coverages" (but not for long-term care services).

In addition, the limited-purpose Health FSA or HRA may pay or reimburse for preventive care benefits.

B. HSA with Suspended HRA

A suspended HRA does not pay or reimburse any medical expense incurred during the suspension period except preventive care, permitted insurance, and permitted coverage (if otherwise allowed to be paid or reimbursed by the HRA).

When the suspension period ends the individual is again entitled to receive payment or reimbursement of section 213(d) medical expenses from the HRA. An individual who does not forgo the payment or reimbursement of medical expenses incurred during an HRA suspension period, is not an eligible individual for HSA purposes during that HRA coverage period.

C. HSA with Post-Deductible Health FSA or HRA

A post-deductible health FSA or HRA does not pay or reimburse any medical expense incurred before the minimum annual deductible is satisfied. The individual would then be an eligible individual for the purpose of making contributions to the HSA.

The deductible for the HRA or health FSA ("other coverage") need not be the same as the deductible for the HDHP, but in no event may the HDHP or other coverage provide benefits before the minimum annual deductible is satisfied.

Where the HDHP and the other coverage do not have identical deductibles, contributions to the HSA are limited to the lower of the deductibles. In addition, although the deductibles of the HDHP and the other coverage may be satisfied independently by separate expenses, no benefits may be paid before the minimum annual HSA deductible has been satisfied.

D. HSA with Retirement HRA

A retirement HRA pays or reimburses only those medical expenses incurred after retirement (and no expenses incurred before retirement). In this case, the individual is an eligible individual for the purpose of making contributions to the HSA before retirement but loses eligibility for coverage periods when the retirement HRA may pay or reimburse section 213(d) medical expenses.

Thus, after retirement, the individual is no longer an eligible individual for the purpose of the HSA. In the arrangements described, the individual does not fail to be an eligible individual under IRS Section 223 and may contribute to an HSA.

In addition, combinations of these arrangements which are consistent with these requirements would not disqualify an individual from being an eligible individual. For example, if an employer offers a combined post-deductible HRA and a limited-purpose health FSA, this would not disqualify an otherwise eligible individual from contributing to an HSA.

Chapter 15

Health Management – Prevention
The Promise of Health

A. Definition

Wellness is a proactive organized program providing lifestyle and medical/clinical assistance to employees and their family members in maintaining good health. Wellness programs encourage voluntary behavior changes and support compliance with proven approaches to maintain health, reduce health risks and enhance individual productivity.

Both PwC and UBA surveys (shown below) indicate that larger companies are more likely to implement health management programs. Each organization surveys their respective client bases and contacts. The survey populations are not identical, but the direction of more health management programs by group size is consistent.

PricewaterhouseCoopers Health & Wellbeing Surveys				
Percentage of Companies Offering Health Management Programs By Company Size and By Year				
Year	<1000 Ees	1000-5000 Ees	5000+ Ees	Total
2016	62%	81%	89%	76%
2015	62%	79%	84%	73%
2014	57%	81%	83%	71%
2013	57%	71%	85%	68%
2012	56%	76%	85%	72%
2011	52%	81%	88%	73%
2010	65%	73%	85%	76%
Source: PwC Health & Wellbeing Surveys				

United Benefit Advisors Health Plan Surveys						
Percentage of Companies Offering Health Management Programs By Company Size and By Year						
Year	<25 Ees	25-49 Ees	50-99 Ees	100-199 Ees	200-499 Ees	500-999 Ees	1000+ Ees
2016	6.1%	10.9%	16.7%	24.9%	35.6%	51.1%	60.3%
2015	6.8%	10.2%	16.2%	26.3%	33.8%	56.3%	61.9%
2014	8.0%	10.0%	16.5%	24.3%	35.5%	50.9%	58.5%
Source: United Benefit Advisors Health Plan Surveys						

Good health management in HCs typically consist of prevention, early intervention, wellness, well-being, and mindfulness.

B. Wellness Programs

The charts below show the year by year growth for each of these common wellness programs:
1. Smoking Cessation
2. Weight Management
3. Fitness/exercise/health clubs
4. Bio-metric Screening
5. Health Risk Appraisals (Wellness Assessments)

Percentage of Companies Offering: Smoking Cessation			
Year	PwC	Kaiser	
		3-199 Ee's	200+ Ee's
2016	73%	37%	74%
2015	66%	41%	71%
2014	63%	26%	64%
2013	61%	39%	71%
2012	61%	28%	70%
2011		31%	63%
2010	71%	23%	60%
2009	64%	28%	61%
2008		19%	59%

Percentage of Companies Offering: Weight Loss Program			
Year	PwC	Kaiser	
		3-99 Ee's	200+ Ee's
2016	64%	33%	68%
2015	59%	39%	61%
2014	53%	18%	48%
2013	52%	31%	58%
2012	52%		
2011			
2010	64%		
2009	63%		
2008			

Percentage of Companies Offering: On-site Fitness, Gym, Exercise			
Year	PwC	Kaiser	
		3-199 Ee's	200+ Ee's
2016	53%		
2015	47%		
2014	42%	26%	64%
2013	38%	21%	69%
2012	38%	28%	65%
2011		29%	64%
2010		29%	63%
2009		27%	63%
2008		22%	60%

Percentage of Companies Offering: Bio-metric Screening			
Year	PwC	Kaiser	
		3-99 Ee's	200+ Ee's
2016	77%	20%	53%
2015	82%	13%	50%
2014	78%	26%	51%
2013		26%	55%
2012			48%
2011			
2010	63%		
2009			
2008			

Percentage of Companies Offering: Health Risk Appraisals						
Year	PwC	Kaiser		Mercer		
		3-199 Ee's	200+ Ee's	10-499 Ee's	500+4999 Ee's	500+ Ee's
2016	80%	32%	59%			
2015	80%	18%	50%		75%	
2014	76%	32%	51%		78%	
2013	80%	23%	55%	36%	73%	78%
2012	80%	18%	38%			

Sources: PwC Health & Wellbeing Surveys
    Kaiser Family Foundation Employee Health Benefits, Annual Surveys
    Mercer's National Survey of Employer Sponsored Health Plans

Other health management programs typically offered are:

Percentage of Companies Offering Various Types of Health Management Programs by Year and Size of Company							
Year	Kaiser				Mercer		
	Wellness Newsletter		Web-based Healthy Living		Nurse Advice Line		Health Advocate	
	3-199 Ee's	200+ Ee's	3-199 Ee's	200+ Ee's	10-499 Ee's	500+ Ee's	10-499 Ee's	500+ Ee's
2016			36%	73%				
2015			39%	68%		71%		56%
2014	33%	60%	38%	77%		69%		52%
2013	47%	60%	47%	78%	51%	80%	30%	51%
2012	45%	62%	45%	77%				
2011	42%	61%	47%	78%	53%	80%	30%	52%
2010	43%	60%	49%	80%				
2009	34%	59%	34%	79%				
2008	27%	51%	32%	69%				

Source: Kaiser/HRET Survey of Employer-Sponsored Health Benefits
Mercer's National Survey of Employer Sponsored Health Plans

Employers can support the use and effectiveness of these programs by:

1. Communication and awareness (newsletters, health fair, posters, local wellness champions)
2. Screening (health awareness profiles, blood pressure check, blood tests, body fat analysis)
3. Health Literacy Education (seminars/classes, self help kits, group discussions, lunch and learn)
4. Behavioral Change (on-site fitness center, flu shots, lunchtime walks, yoga classes)

C. Well-being Programs

Many plans are expanding and evolving traditional wellness programs into well-being initiatives. Well-being focuses on the person both at work and outside of work. Well-being lifestyle programs and classes can include areas such as:

1. Financial education
2. Family counseling
3. Child rearing
4. Homemaking
5. Spiritual guidance
6. Leadership training
7. Team building
8. Creative thinking
9. Auto mechanics
10. Pet caring

D. The Need for Health Management - <u>Video 113</u>

There is clearly a medical, organizational, and social need and reason health management programs are popular. Surveys show that for every 100 members:

o   23-30% smoke (70% want to quit, 35% try each year)
o   29% have high blood pressure
o   30% have cardiovascular disease
o   80% do not exercise regularly
o   55% or more are overweight or obese
o   30% are prone to low back pain (many linked to obesity)
o   6-9% have diabetes
o   10% are depressed
o   35% are under significant stress

E. The Desire for Health Management

Health management programs have grown rapidly partly due to the receptivity of plan members to accept help. Surveys indicate that for every 100 members:

- o 47% are trying to improve their diet
- o 37% plan to undergo some health screening
- o 30% state they exercise regularly
- o Only 23% are aware of the health promotion and wellness programs offered by their employer sponsored health plans
- o 76% of employers with over 11,000 employees offer health management programs

F. Impacting Plan Members

Effective Wellness Programs

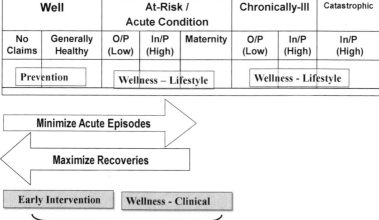

Well		At-Risk / Acute Condition			Chronically-Ill		Catastrophic
No Claims	Generally Healthy	O/P (Low)	In/P (High)	Maternity	O/P (Low)	In/P (High)	In/P (High)
Prevention		Wellness – Lifestyle			Wellness - Lifestyle		

Minimize Acute Episodes

Maximize Recoveries

Early Intervention   Wellness - Clinical

Traditional Wellness Programs

The key is to develop health management programs that minimize acute episodes by supporting and encouraging prevention, wellness and lifestyle changes for those already healthy.

When a plan member does have an acute illness, minor hospitalization, or a maternity stay, the important actions are to maximize recovery by providing early intervention, timely treatments, and effective clinical care. Getting individuals recovered and back to a healthy state as soon as possible will benefit the plan member and save treatment costs from complications.

G. Key Decisions

1. Will the wellness program be for employees only or employees and dependents?
2. Will you purchase from vendor, internally develop, or integrate a combination?
3. Consider in conjunction with plan covered wellness benefits (immunizations, mammograms, screening, EAP, physical exams, pre-natal care, well child care, etc.)
4. Consider in conjunction with worksite programs (safety, ergonomics, work-life programs, etc.)
5. What incentives/rewards will be provided for compliance or penalties for non-compliance?

H. Prevention

Prevention has three distinct segments:

1. **Primary Prevention** is aimed at preventing the on-set of disease. Examples: Immunizations, annual physicals, and promotion of physical activity.

2. **Secondary Prevention** is aimed at treating a disease after its onset, but before it causes serious complications. Examples: Identifying individuals at risk for diabetes, hypertension, heart disease and providing early intervention.

3. **Tertiary Prevention** is aimed at treating the late or final stages so as to minimize the degree of disability and improve functionality.

I. Preventive Coverage under the ACA

The ACA requires that all insurance companies that are not grandfathered and all new plans sold must cover preventive services without cost-sharing requirements that:

1. are graded "A" or "B" by the U.S. Preventive Services Task Force (USPSTF),
2. cover certain immunizations;
3. cover preventive services for infants, children, adolescents and women as provided in guidelines developed by HHS's Health Resources and Services Administration.

While the USPSTF is the main source for identifying clinically proved value of preventive care services through their A&B recommendations, the actual law includes other sources for recommending, developing and maintaining the list of required services. The following are entities that can directly impact the inclusion of preventive coverages under the ACA:

(1) United States Preventive Services Task Force: evidence-based items or services that have a recommendation rating of 'A' or 'B'

(2) Advisory Committee on Immunization Practices of the Centers for Disease Control and Prevention immunizations: recommendations from the (ACIP/CDC Immunization website), and

(3) Health Resources and Services Administration (HRSA):
    a. with respect to <u>infants, children,</u> and <u>adolescents,</u> evidence-informed preventive care and screenings
    b. with respect to <u>women,</u> such additional preventive care and screenings not otherwise described.

USPSTF methods have evolved over time. The USPSTF evaluates the quality and strength of the evidence for the service, the net health benefit (benefit minus harms) associated with the service, and the level of certainty that this level of benefit will be realized if these services are provided in a primary care setting.

The USPSTF will continue to affect coverages provided because of the unbiased scientific studies they perform identifying the value of specific preventive care options. This process is outlined in the Agency for Health Research and Quality (AHRQ Procedure Manual, which can be found at: http://www.ahrq.gov/clinic/uspstf08/methods/procmanual.htm

Many employers and insurance plans will likely follow or seriously consider the USPSTF recommendations whether or not mandated by any federal or state law.

Video 113

Chapter 16

Condition Management – <u>Video 114</u>

A. Definition

Condition/Disease Management is a proactive organized program providing lifestyle and medical/clinical assistance to employees and their family members with chronic and persistent conditions.

Condition management programs encourage voluntary behavior changes and support compliance with proven medical practices which stabilize conditions, reduce health risks and enhance their individual productivity.

B. High Cost Claims

Condition Management Potential Focus on Hi-Volume / Hi-Cost Users

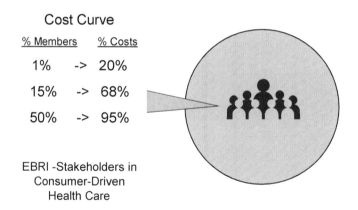

Cost Curve

% Members		% Costs
1%	->	20%
15%	->	68%
50%	->	95%

EBRI -Stakeholders in Consumer-Driven Health Care

The Employee Benefit Research Institute (EBRI) estimates that on average 68% of claim costs come from 15% of the covered population. The high cost claims are good targets for condition management interventions.

While many employers are focusing on health management and wellness, condition management represents an opportunity to help those in significant distress with major illnesses and to lower costs through compliance and lifestyle support to minimize complications and hospitalizations. For example, a stabilized diabetic has about 1/6th lower costs from fewer complications and fewer hospitalizations.

C. Impacting Plan Members

Effective Condition Management

Well		At-Risk / Acute Condition			Chronically-Ill		Catastrophic
No Claims	Generally Healthy	O/P (Low)	In/P (High)	Maternity	O/P (Low)	In/P (High)	In/P (High)
Prevention		Wellness – Lifestyle			Wellness - Lifestyle		

Minimize Complications

Maximize Stabilization

Wellness - Clinical

Condition Management Programs

The key is to develop condition management programs that minimize complications by supporting and encouraging wellness and lifestyle changes for those with chronic and persistent conditions.

When a plan member does have an emergency room or hospitalization the important actions are to provide quick and effective clinical care and provide education on any wellness and lifestyle changes to maximize stabilization and avoid future re-hospitalizations.

D. Elements of Condition Management

There are four elements of a successful condition/disease management program:

1. *A delivery system of health care* professionals and organizations closely coordinating to provide medical care and support the patient's compliance throughout the course of a disease.
2. *A process that monitors* the compliance and describes outcome-based care guidelines for targeted patients.
3. *A process for continuous improvement* that measures clinical behavior, refines treatment standards, and improves the quality of care provided.
4. *Incentives/penalties* that support the condition management medical and clinical care services.

E. The Need for Condition Management

There is clearly a NEED for condition management as evidenced in several industry surveys that show:

- 60+% of an employer's total medical costs come from chronic and persistent diseases.
- 45% of Americans live with at least one chronic disease. 14% live with two or more chronic diseases.
- 76% of hospitalizations, 72% of physician visits, and 88% of Rx is due to chronic conditions.
- The average cost of health care for a diabetic is $13,200/yr compared to $2,600/yr for a non-diabetic.
- 61 million Americans live with cardiovascular disease
- 50% of chronic disease deaths are traced to cardiovascular disease.
- Coronary artery disease is a leading cause of premature permanent disability.
- Obesity is becoming the #1 preventable cause of death.

F. The Desire for Compliance

However, the DESIRE for change among the average patient with one or more chronic conditions is very limited. Education, health literacy, and decision support can have a significant impact on changing the following:

- 70+% of Mental Health patients do not adhere to medication therapies.
- 50% of patients do not follow recommended standards of care.
- 33% with high blood pressure do not know.
- 33% of diabetics do not know it.
- Patient's lack of knowledge and information.
- Patients without financial incentives to change health and healthcare behaviors.
- Distortions of current 3rd party reimbursement medical financing system.
- Plans pay for treatments not prevention or compliance.
- Physicians without incentives to take time and effort to deal effectively with chronic conditions.

G. Financial Alignment

To have a successful condition management program you must design your program intensity and align your vendor payments with your organizational goals. The chart below shows the level of intensity desired in a program and the best vendor relationship to achieve an optimum level of participation and a ROI.

The expected participation can vary from 10-75%. The expected ROI can range up to 3 dollars for every dollar spent.

Condition Management Programs
Designed and Financially Aligned for Success

Program Type:	Passive	Assertive	Aggressive
	Phone and mail out- reach, no incentives	Incentives (i.e., waiving Rx copays)	Incentives (i.e, waiving Rx copays, premium differential
DM vendor pricing method	Per employee per month, all employees	Low PEPM on all ees plus hourly or per case rate on participants only (rate varies based on participant risk status)	Low PEPM on all ees plus hourly or per case rate on participants only (rate varies based on participant risk status)
Percentage of chronic diseased participating in program	10%	50%	75%
Return on investment of disease management programs	0 - .5	1.5 - 2	1.5 - 3

H. Condition Management by Generation (Revisited)

Below is a summary of condition management comments presented in separate previous generational chapters of this video-text book.

1st generation HC - Condition management is not a major focus of 1st generation HC. This led to the early criticisms that such plans were only for the young and healthy. 1stgeneration condition management features include basic healthcare information, access to an online health coach, and call-center based specific disease support programs.

2nd generation HC – Condition management programs have lagged behind providing rewards like many do for health management. There has been limited experience and a lack of consensus for determining ROI and the impact on managing chronic and persistent diseases and conditions. The most effective programs for condition management seem to focus on a limited number of conditions and combine that focus with information and financial incentives.

3rdgeneration HC – the focus of condition management on impacting not only health and healthcare costs, but corporate metrics, such as: productivity, absenteeism, disability, turnover, unscheduled sick leave, presenteeism, and worker's compensation. Aggregate survey information and population management tools like Wellness Assessments can direct an employer's education and work-site assistance efforts.

4th generation HC - Condition management considers culturally sensitive disease management, measures individual outcomes, and supports personal health status. These condition management programs focus on compliance, adherence, and monitoring of mental and physical health concerns. Patients with heart conditions, diabetes, COPD, and asthma will find life saving alerts and rapid provider responses to changes in vital signs. Patients with apnea will have sleep patterns and disruptions monitored. The efficacy of equipment and treatment plans will be tuned to personal needs.

5th generation HC - For disease or condition management programs, the emphasis will shift from recovery to functionality. It will no longer be acceptable to simply eliminate symptoms or use traditional medical treatments to deal with chronic conditions. Key personal relationships will develop as "friendship pods." 5th generation HC plans will formulate, connect and encourage mentoring and "Wisemen" counsels to help others in need. Methodist structures similar to its "Steven's Ministry" will create neighbor to neighbor health support and palliative listening leaders.

I. Industry Surveys on Condition Managements Implementations

The table below shows that large groups (5000+ employees) have embraced condition management programs much more aggressively than have smaller employers (fewer than 1000 employees).

Percentage of Companies Offering Condition Management Programs By Year and Size				
Year	<1000 Ees	1000-5000 Ees	5000+ Ees	All Sizes
2016	32%	61%	80%	56%
2015	39%	64%	76%	57%
2014	31%	64%	79%	53%
2013	31%	60%	75%	49%
2012	28%	65%	81%	58%
2011	40%	74%	86%	66%
2010	41%	68%	83%	68%
Source: PwC Health & Wellbeing Surveys				

Percentage of Companies Offering Types of Condition Management Programs by Year and Size				
Year	Case Management		Disease Management	
	10-499 Ee's	500+ Ee's	10-499 Ee's	500+ Ee's
2015				83%
2014				80%
2013	34%	82%	42%	80%
2012				
2011	35%	83%	42%	82%
Source: Mercer's National Survey of Employer Sponsored Health Plans				

Percentage of Companies Offering Selected Condition Management Programs By Year							
Year	Diabetes	Asthma	Cardiac	COPD	Hyper tension	Cancer	Depression
2016	73%	55%	58%	55%	30%	47%	34%
2015	93%	74%	76%	74%	67%	62%	48%
2014	72%	57%	56%	53%	48%	42%	34%
2013	70%	59%	57%	54%		46%	35%
Source: PwC Health & Wellness Touchstone Survey							

Conclusions:

1. Case management and disease management programs are offered by over 80% of companies with 500 or more employees, nearly twice the rate of companies with 10-499 employees.

2. Continuing the pattern with implementing consumerism programs, large groups lead the way with 80% (5000 or more employees) offering Condition Management versus 32% for smaller groups (under 1000 employees).

3. The top 5 conditions provided in condition management programs are diabetes (73%), Asthma (55%), Cardiac (58%), COPD (55%), and cancer (47%).

Video 114

Chapter 17

Health Literacy / Decision Support
The Promise of Transparency

Health literacy and effective decision support tools are the "soft underbelly" of HC. Creating smart patients lags behind the other building blocks of HC. If this area of current weakness is not resolved properly and/or if plan sponsors do not emphasize and support health literacy in materials and actions, HC may fail.

To be successful, HC should have extensive educational, information, and decision support tools. The plan member needs help with product selections and patients need support with clinical options, cost concerns, and lifestyle decisions. These tools serve as the foundation for encouraging behavioral changes by helping individuals make informed health care and medical treatment decisions. Information is intended to supplement the patient/physician relationship, and provide a level of understanding about a potential or proposed course of treatment.

Decision aids help to shape consumers' knowledge of the benefits and patients understanding the risks of each treatment option. With improved knowledge of expected outcomes, consumers using decision guides have been more actively involved and effective in making decisions as partners with their doctors.

Five compelling points underline why consumer decision guides are an integral part of the HC process.

1. ***Patients as Consumers want information—and control.*** They want to pick their health plans, doctors, and treatments; they want information, options, and involvement.
2. ***Patients as Consumers use and like decision aids.*** When offered and effectively communicated, people use them and find them helpful.

3. *Decision aids change minds.* When personal choice plays a critical role or patients are undecided about their options, decision aids are particularly useful.
4. *Decision aids improve the quality of care and lower costs.* Informed medical decisions can reduce unnecessary visits and services, increase use of highly effective services, and ultimately lower costs.
5. *Decision aids are getting smarter.* Use of prescribed decision aids have become increasingly effective as health plans use predictive modelling to identify specific opportunities to support smart decision making.

Measure	Related Health Issue	% of Consumers that Don't Know	% that WANT to Know
Blood Pressure	Health Risks & Chronic Conditions	68%	85%
Cholesterol	Access to Clinical Data	81%	80%
Blood Sugar A1c	Medical Reminders	83%	65%
Body Mass Index	Tracking Goals	79%	56%
Know None	Want Help Setting Personal Goals	89%	55%
Source: HealthMine			

Health Literacy by Generation (Revisited)

Below is a summary of health literacy comments presented in separate chapters of this video-text book.

1st Generation Decision Support

1st generation decision support services focus on providing members information on discretionary expenses, such as, prescription drugs costs, relative office visits costs, plan comparison cost calculators, and basic clinical library information.

Consumer information tools help individuals assess the relative value of purchases, whether paid for personally or covered by their medical plan. Such tools may help individuals:

- Compare benefit plans
- Evaluate wellness, wellbeing, and preventive care lifestyle changes
- Locate in-network providers
- Select alternative prescription drugs based on cost and efficacy
- Evaluate the risks and benefits of expensive procedures or tests
- Compare providers based on quality indicators
- Understand acute and chronic conditions and how best to manage them

2nd Generation Decision Support

Appropriate content, form of messages, and good programs and tools are necessary but not sufficient to change consumer and health behaviors. 2nd generation decision support tools that focus on changing health and consumer behaviors require active patient involvement with learning, practice, reinforcement, and rewards. Although measurement of the value of behavioral changes can be challenging, collection and evaluation of program metrics is essential.

The road to providing education and support tools is neither an easy nor a short path. A Kaiser Foundation study of how consumers compare the quality of health care among different providers showed that they would first seek a friend or family member, followed by a health care professional. At the bottom of the list fell published materials and a toll-free number. More recently, health consumers have shown a strong interest in web tools. Smart phone technology and readily available phone apps are easy and convenient sources of medical information. Be sure that plan members are provided the right tools consistent with the plan design and coverages.

Without question, HC requires significant effort and responsibility from individuals. They must make decisions about how they want to spend their healthcare dollars, which providers to see, and what services are necessary. Both proponents and critics agree that success depends on members making good health and healthcare decisions based on medical evidence, personal preferences, and overall value. For HC to ultimately succeed within an organization, it must put interactive action-based health decision tools into the hands of its members. Below is a listing of typical decision support tools.

Basic Design Information
        HRA Fund Accounting
        Underlying PPO Plan Design
        Disease and/or Medical Management
        HSA Fund Accounting
        Debit/Credit Card

Personal Benefit Support
        Plan Comparison Cost Estimator
        Account Balance
        On-line Claim Inquiry
        Summary Plan Description

Personal Health Management
    Health Risk Appraisal
    Health & Wellness Information
    Targeted Health Content
    Medical Record, History
    Health Coach

Provider Selection Support
    Physician Quality Comparison
    Physician Cost Comparison
    Hospital Quality Comparison
    Hospital Cost Comparison

Care Support
    On-line Provider Directory
    Provider Scheduling
    On-line Rx Comparisons
    On-line Patient Decision Support
    24/7 Nurse Line

3rd Generation Decision Support Tools

3rd generation tools extend the impact of decision support tools to other health, safety, and performance metrics of an organization. Aggregated claim and risk assessment data can serve as the foundation to help identify opportunities for ongoing improvement in the health needs of the employed population. Targeted information, assessment, self-help and interventions in areas such as stress relief though lifestyle change and work process changes can have a dramatic impact on health & performance. In addition, organizational resources (other compensation, safety, and recognition programs) may be better leveraged to optimally engage and support the employee's health, well-being, and productivity.

For example, there can be an integration of and hot links to HR programs of financial management, leadership training, family support programs, and other corporate self-help and training.

4th Generation Decision Support Tools

4th generation decision support tools will focus on the individual needs of each member. As 4th generation concepts develop, vendors can provide "arrive in time" information and services at critical moments for care. "Information therapy" as promoted by Healthwise suggests the active use of patient oriented information with clinical evidence based medicine. Information needs to be embedded into the process of care—as information therapy.

"Information therapy" is the prescription of specific, evidence-based medical information to a patient, caregiver, or consumer at just the right time to help that person make a specific health decision or behavior change. It is the ultimate consumer decision support aid.

For example, Healthwise identifies potential of "prescribing decision support" aids for each of the following tests and treatments:

1. Prostate surgery
2. Back surgery
3. ACL surgery
4. Coronary artery bypass surgery
5. Medication for depression
6. End-of-life care
7. Prescription of beta-blockers following heart attacks
8. Early-stage breast cancer testing
9. Colon cancer screenings
10. Immunizations and eye test reminders for diabetics

Information is powerful if used as an important part of medical care and if supported with incentives and part of a value chain for treatment. If properly integrated into care, it can be as important to health and healthcare as a medical test, medication, or treatment. With good information people can achieve better health outcomes at lower costs. With good information consumers will be better equipped to fully accept their role in the new world of HC.

Chapter 18

Incentives & Rewards
The Promise of Shared Savings

Any strategy to motivate behavior changes must include two elements – education and incentives. Employers have been providing education and decision support tools for many years. Incentive strategies have been slower to develop. Initially, incentives may seem like additional costs with an uncertain return. But for the foreseeable future, positive and negative financial incentives represent the "secret sauce" that optimizes engagement and makes HC work.

Employers are finding that motivating employees to better health and healthcare choices is complicated. Companies start with different histories, cultures, demographics, educational backgrounds, and lifestyle interests. The need for behavior change to improve health is well established. The Centers for Disease Control studies show that 50% of health status is determined by personal behaviors. – **Video 114**

Determinants of Health				
60%				
50%				
40%				
30%				
20%				
10%				
Determinants	**Access to Health**	**Genetics**	**Environment**	**Behavior**
Percentage	**10%**	**20%**	**20%**	**50%**
Source: CDC, Centers for Disease Control				

Providing incentives is about helping people to get or stay healthy. When done properly, it can lower costs. If that is accomplished, the healthier individual wins with improved health and the employer wins with a productive workforce.

The evidence showing the value of incentives is clear. Incentives may be the missing link to greater voluntary participation, healthier habits and lower costs. A study by Health2Resources stated that almost two-thirds of U.S. companies offer programs to keep employees healthy. Sixty-six percent offering programs use incentives, with many showing a return on investment greater than $1 for each dollar spent.

A key finding in their study was that the value of incentives increase each year. Amounts range from $1 per pound for weight loss to over $1,500 in annual premium reductions. The most common incentive is health premium reduction, followed by merchandise or tokens and gift cards.

Incentives have been evolving from rewards for just participation in activities to health outcomes based on selected metrics. A survey by Towers Watson found that 42% of large firms   require employees to complete health coaching or a disease management program in order to earn a financial incentive. And, 17% said they either had in place or were considering plans in which employees' health status would have to improve or be maintained. That is, they would have to meet established targets for body mass index (BMI), blood pressure (BP) or cholesterol levels, or show improvement towards those goals to earn their reward.

Self reported data has proven to be too inaccurate. Information from medical professionals and lab tests are developing as the standard. In 2011, 40% of employers offered incentives based on bio-metrics, which can include tested results for blood pressure, blood sugar, cholesterol, body mass index (BMI), A1c levels, and waist size.

These approaches to consumerism focus on empowering individuals with information and a financial stake in their own health and healthcare. A key feature of HC is providing individuals with opportunities to be financially rewarded for doing the right activities that improve their health. With the expansion of successful incentive strategies member participation is dramatically higher and results are much improved.

For example, <u>Bravo Wellness</u> offers employers several options to use bio-metric based incentives. Their clients have experienced above 90% participation rates. They offer a full range of incentives including participation in a wellness assessment, attending a smoking cessation class, compliance with a condition management program (e.g. taking medications, diet, exercise, office visits), and maintenance of good health characteristics or bio-metrics (e.g. blood pressure, cholesterol, nicotine use, body mass index). They have found that the best results are third party verified bio-metrics.

In another example, a large U.S. employer incentivized employees to get an annual physical. Since participation in onsite biometrics screenings had been very low for many years, the company decided to eliminate onsite screens and, instead, invest in a year-round communication campaign about the importance of establishing a relationship with a primary care physician, which can start with an annual physical.

The campaign was targeted toward employees and spouses. The reward for getting an annual physical was a reduction in monthly medical premiums. Participation rates jumped from 29% in the onsite screenings to 75% getting an annual physical. The benefit to the plan members was an established relationship with a PCP, which meant more members adhered to medications and treatment plans as well they avoided costly Emergency Room visits for non-emergencies. The benefit to the employer was reduced costs in the long run and access to more claims data to target members for condition management programs.

The ACA allows incentives for both participation and health outcomes. The ACA increased the maximum for incentives based on health status from 20% to 30% of the cost of coverage. The act allows the Secretary of Health & Human Services to increase health status incentives to 50%.

Financial incentives are critical to changing behaviors. If just being healthy was good enough, we would not have growing rates of diabetes and an epidemic of obesity in this country. We have a typically American attitude. We want to be paid to do the right things. We want financial incentives. Health reform allows current market initiatives and new products to continue to include substantial financial incentives.

Incentives can take on many forms. The chart below describes several options employers can use to engage employees in healthy choices. Both positive and negative incentives are possible. Existing rules allow a combination of incentives and penalties to exist within the same structure as long as the difference between the best and worst financial impact is within federal allowances.

Types of Consumerism Financial Incentives			
Goal of Incentives	**Decision timing**	**Health Status**	**Examples**
Select optional health plans or provider networks that meet the cost and coverage needs of the member.	During open enrollment	Distribution between the healthy and ill reflecting underlying enrollee population.	Premium tiered health plans
Select a low cost, high quality provider	Varies, usually at the point of care	Patient is usually ill or needing service.	Point of care tiered health plans
Select a low cost, high quality treatment option	At the point of care	Usually when the patient becomes ill, sometimes before	Tiered drug benefits Incentives for following Evidence Based care

Types of Consumerism Financial Incentives (continued)			
Goal of Incentives	Decision timing	Health Status	Examples
Reduce health risks by engaging members to seek care.	Ongoing	Varies—the patient has a high risk or chronic condition	Incentives to comply with recommended care (e.g., prenatal care)
Reduce health risks by engaging members to change lifestyle	Ongoing	Varies—the patient has a lifestyle factor that increases health risks	Incentives based on outcomes using Bio-metrics

Source: Consumer Financial Incentives: A Decision Guide for Purchasers, Prepared for: Agency for Healthcare Research and Quality U.S. Department of Health and Human Services, 540 Gaither Road, Rockville, MD 20850 (Some simplifications and modifications made by Ron Bachman)

There are at least five areas that can be changed to implement financial incentives:

1. **Premiums** – this allows both the employee and the employer to share any savings based upon the split in how each contributes to the overall cost of the plan.
2. **Employee Contribution Rate** – this allows greater flexibility to award employees more or less that would occur by using the "change in premium" approach.
3. **Deductible** – increase or decrease the plan deductible based upon compliance standards set in the plan.
4. **Cost-sharing** – this would expand on the "change deductible" approach and impact any combination of deductible, coinsurance, maximum out of pocket costs, and copayments.
5. **Personal Care Accounts** – this would allow direct increases to HSAs or HRAs.

The major areas of differentiation in employment compensation packages may be the provisions for rewards, incentives, and information to support healthy productive employees. Employers will always be concerned about their "human capital." High functioning employees lower the costs of unscheduled sick days, absenteeism, disabilities, workers compensation claims, and improve productivity.

The ACA limits incentive options for coverage offered through the government exchanges. Exchange insurance cannot use incentives to directly impact premiums for employees. For those plans that can use the full capabilities of incentives, financial extras are likely to grow and expand as employers continue to seek ways of controlling health costs and improving productivity.

The strategy of linking employee incentives to results must follow federal rules. When an incentive (or penalty) is contingent upon the satisfaction of health status, a plan must:

- o   Be designed to promote health and wellness
- o   Not exceed 30% of the total cost of coverage offered
- o   Be available to all "similarly situated individuals"
- o   Offer an appeals process
- o   Provide "reasonable alternatives" when appropriate
- o   Offer re-assessments at least once per year

HC with a proper plan design supported by information and incentives has proven itself to lower costs and improve quality of care. The American Academy of Actuaries reports that Healthcare Consumerism lowers costs in the first year by 12-20% and reduces future trend increases about one-half or up to 3-5%.

The great challenge for any employer looking to establish an incentive strategy is to determine what amount of incentive for what activity will work to motivate their employees. Listen to them. Survey them. Look to similar companies in similar industries. It will be an evolutionary process with constant changes and modifications. Be logical, fair and transparent. You may need to start the process with participation incentives and evolve from there to health status rewards. The value of incentives and the type of incentives you choose for your employees is critical. The evidence is mounting. Providing results based incentives seems to lead to better outcomes for both the individual and the plan.

Video 114

Chapter 19

The Patient-Provider Relationship
Video 106

HC at its best will strengthen the patient-provider relationship. An effective plan aligns the interests of the employer, the patient, and the provider of care. The key connection is the patient-provider relationship which is also the most trusted relationship in the health and healthcare system. Too often third party administrators (TPAs) interfere with the effective delivery of care.

In traditional PPO plan designs there are inherent conflicts of interest. Insurers establish networks of providers by first demanding lower charges. Insurers restrict the services for which they reimburse physicians by using limited CPT codes. They restrict how a provider practices medicine to insurer-determined "medically necessary" services.

"Standards of Care" can be different between urban and rural markets, but insurers generally apply a "one size fits all" standard that ignores special situations and individual needs. Wellness benefits, preventive services, and early intervention care is set not by the provider but by third party administrators (e.g. insurers, wellness vendors, or condition management companies).

Changing Roles of Insurers & Providers

Traditional Managed Care Focus on Behavioral Change

Building Blocks	Employer	Plan Member (Consumer)	TPAs, Insurers	Providers
		Behavior Change →	← Restrictions	Conflicts
Personal Care Accounts	Account Options	Create Savings	Administer Accounts	N/A
Health Mgmt	Worksite Wellness	Healthy Lifestyle	Benefit Designs	Prevention, Primary Care
Condition Mgmt	Access to Specialists	Treatment Compliance	Medical Protocols	Standards of Care
Health Literacy	Multi-Media Campaigns	Education	Decision Tools	Medical Counsel
Incentives	Financier	Pay for Compliance	Administer Payments	Pay for Performance
Consumerism Focus	Facilitator, Coordinator	Empowered Responsible	Enabler	Care Manager

CONFUSION

The focus of traditional PPO plan designs and programs is to "change plan member behaviors." Those PPOs follow a "managed care" model that many times seem to just manage costs through restrictions and limitations. Even following HC the focus is on behavior change and engagement, but as directed mainly by the TPAs and/or insurers.

In this model, the TPA/Insurers are focused on applying rules and restrictions to the care of plan members. Whether it is health management, condition management, health literacy, or incentives - the third party administrators (TPAs) generally control the benefits. They do what they believe is needed to help the member stay healthy, get healthy, or stabilize a medical condition. Too often the treatment opinions recommended by care providers are dismissed or ignored. The provider of care is left to navigate the different rules of different carriers and TPAs.

The dark arrow between the TPAs/Insurers and the providers show the potential for conflicts in achieving the desired medical care.

For example, providers may want to include preventive care that is not otherwise covered. He/she may want to provide screening or educational sessions on health or healthcare that are not reimbursed. While inefficient and rife with conflicts, this is the most common structure used by health plans.

The more effective HC model reverses the position of the providers and the TPAs. In this model, the emphasis is on strengthening the patient-provider relationship by creating a system that emphasizes the judgments of the provider over the insurer. After all, for large self-insured employer sponsored health plans, the insurer is simply a processor of claims. The employer and provider should be setting the rules for what is covered and what treatments are needed, and what is not.

Changing Roles of Insurers & Providers
Integrated Healthcare Focus on Patient-Provider Relationship

Building Blocks	Employer	Plan Member (Patient)	Providers	TPAs,
Behavior Change Engagement			Effective Care	Communication
Personal Care Accounts	Account Options	Create Savings	N/A	Administer Accounts
Health Mgmt	Worksite Wellness	Healthy Lifestyle	Prevention Primary Care	Benefit Designs
Condition Mgmt	Access to Specialists	Treatment Compliance	Standards Care	Medical Protocols
Health Literacy	Multi-Media Campaigns	Education	Medical Counsel	Decision Tools
Incentives	Pay for Risk	Pay for Compliance	Pay for Performance	Pay for Admin.
Patient-Centered Focus	Accountable Plans, Coordinator	Acct'able Health	Acct'able Care	Acct'able Administration

(Cooperation)

Employers can contract directly with physicians to care for plan members. Direct contracting and concierge services are growing segments. While TPAs can be very rigid in how they will process claims, employers need to be more assertive in demanding TPAs pay for medical services based on what the employers and providers of care agree is needed for a healthy workforce.

Companies such as MedEncentive have developed software that encourages and rewards the post-office visit continuation of care. Both patient and provider are rewarded for follow up actions and educational feedback regarding care.

With a change of approach, insurers can restructure their approach to building provider networks. By working cooperatively with providers, insurers can improve the patient-provider relationship.

Some Integrated Delivery Systems (IDS) like InterMountain Health, Kaiser-Permanente (California), and a few Accountable Care Organizations (ACOs) are examples of systems that can utilize the HC plan designs and strengthen the patient-provider relationship.

The focus on the patient-provider relation is gaining steam as we move from health insurance reform to real healthcare reform. Look to how the patient-provider relationship is strengthened with each new program or addition made to your existing HC programs.

This model works best for self-insured plans because in those cases the employer is taking the risk of claim costs and use. Employers can set the rules and require TPAs to abide by them and reimburse for services designed and priced by the employer-provider relations. In some cases, this can lead to fixed bundled pricing for certain conditions such as diabetes and mental health.

Video 106

Chapter 20

Cost Savings - <u>Video 118</u>

The potential cost savings for implementing HC can be significant. Of course, it will depend on where you are starting the process and what level of efficient HC strategies is being implemented. Cost savings of thirty percent or more are possible.

Potential Savings from Healthcare Consumerism				
Gross* Savings as Percentage of Total Plan Costs				
Effective Programs Implemented	... Traditional Plans.... ....Healthcare Consumerism Plans...........			
Basic	**Passive**	**1st Generation**	**2nd Generation**	**3rd + Generation & Future**
Expanded	2%	3%	7%	10%
Complete	3-4%	6-8%	12-15%	20+ %
Comprehensive (Future)	5%	10%	20%	30%
* Excludes Carry-over HRAs/HSAs and any added administrative costs of specialized programs				

The early chapters of this book outlined the need for establishing basic principles, an HR benefits vision consistent with the organization's vision, and acceptable strategies. When done properly those initial steps will lead to programs that are in alignment with the organizational needs and the needs of its members.

Strategically it is usually best to move gradually but with a long term 3-5 year plan. There are lots of potential programs that vendors will sell. It is best to select those programs that will align with the long term HC strategies. (See chapter on "The Formula for Change").

How ingrained and aggressive those selected programs will be can determine if the optimum success is achieved. The chart of "Potential Savings" shows how effective programs and evolving generations of HC can lower costs with plan members making better health and healthcare decisions.

Video 118

Year after year studies have shown the cost reduction potential and the health improving value of account-based plans. Below is a sampling of such studies over several years.

A. 2016 Mercer survey: Health benefit cost growth slows to 2.4% in 2016 as enrollment in high-deductible plans climbs

Coverage in an HSA eligible HDHP costs 22% less, on average, than coverage in a traditional PPO plan among large employers, even when employer contributions to employee HSA accounts are included. Adding HDHPs has been a key strategy for employers concerned about the ACA's excise tax on high-cost plans. The largest employers have moved the fastest. Among organizations with 20,000+ employees, 80% offered an HDHP and enrollment jumped from 29% to 40% of all covered employees in 2016.

B. *2015 National Bureau of Economic Research - 3 Year study*

The study, which analyzed data from 13 million individuals in 54 large U.S. firms, determined that health care cost growth among employers offering CDHPs is significantly lower in each of the first three years after implementation, validating that the plans have a compounding impact on overall employer health plan cost savings. According to the study, annual health care spending for companies with CDHPs was on average 6.6 percent lower in the first year post-implementation, compared to organizations with traditional plans. The cost increase differential changed to 4.3 percent after year two, and 3.4 percent after year three.

C. 2014 Aon Hewitt Health Care Survey

From 2012 to 2013, health care trend abated somewhat, with employers reporting 5 percent trend overall (all plans combined); PPO models experienced 5 percent trend, with 4 percent for HDHP's with HSA and only 3 percent for CDHP's with HRA

D. 2011 Rand Corp Study

The largest-ever assessment of high-deductible health plans finds that while such plans significantly cut health spending, they also prompt patients to cut back on preventive health care, according to a 2011 RAND Corporation study.

Studying more than 800,000 families from across the United States, researchers found that when people shifted into health insurance plans with high deductibles, their health spending dropped an average of 14 percent when compared to families in health plans with lower deductibles.

Health care spending also was lower among families enrolled in high-deductible plans that had moderate health savings accounts sponsored by employers.

E. 2009 American Academy of Actuaries Consumerism Studies

1st Year Savings: The total savings generated could be as much as 12 percent to 20 percent in the first year.
  - All studies showed a drop in costs in the first year of a CDHP plan from -4 percent to -15 percent. A control population of traditional plans experienced increases of +8 percent to +9 percent.
  – 2+ Year Savings: At least two of the studies indicate trend rates lower than traditional PPO plans by approximately 3 percent to 5 percent.
  - If these lower trends can be further validated, it will represent a substantial cost-reduction strategy for employers and employees.
  – Cost Shifting: The studies indicated that while the possibility for employer cost-shifting exists with CDHP plans, (as it does with traditional plans) most employers are not doing so, and might even be reducing employee cost-sharing under certain circumstances.

Chapter 21

Implementing
Healthcare Consumerism
<u>Video 117</u>

There are many different ways to implement HC. An organization may have the necessary resources and skills within its HR department. It may want to engage an insurer/TPA for coordinating implementation. It may select an independent 3rd party to act as a "general manager." The organization may even use a private exchange to coordinate its consumerism strategies.

Creating an implementation process and selecting the right partner(s) should reflect the organization's intent to either select separate "best practice" vendors or go with a single source integrated package of services.

The following chart is presented as a framework for a long term multi-year implementation. Simply estimate within a 3-5 year strategy those areas the organization seeks to implement. Start with the generations. Plans will likely include aspects of many generations simultaneously. The dates to fill in at the top are the years that the organization expects to target an introduction of some aspects of that generation.

The dates across from each building block and beneath each generation should likewise be filled in as the year targeted for implementing that specific area of HC.

Once completed, the mapping of the strategy with future target dates should provide a good general plan for measuring progress and making future adjustments, HR planning, and vendor selections.

	Yr	Yr	Yr	Yr	Yr
The HC Grid	**1st Gen** Health & Discretion Expenses	**2nd Gen** Behavior Changes, Shared Savings	**3rd Gen** Integrated Health & Performance	**4th Gen** Personal Care	**5th Gen** Community Health & Productive Longevity
Personal Care Accounts	Initial Account Only	Activity & Compliance Rewards	Indiv. & Grp Corporate Metric Rewards	Specialized Accts, Matching HRAs, Expanded QMEs	Volunteer Vessels, Pay Forward, Charitable Giving
Year ->					
Wellness & Health Mgmt	100% ACA Mandated Preventive Care	Web-based Behavior Change Support	Worksite Wellnes, on-site clinics, safety, Stress & Error reduction	Genomics Predictive Modelling Push Technology	Natural Resource Flows, Longevity more than Health
Year->					
Disease & Condition Mgmt	Information, Health Coach	Disease Specific Compliance Awards	Population Mgmt, IHM, Integrated Back-to-Work	Wire-less support, Cultural DM, Holistic Care	Functionality, Community, Faith & Spirituality
Year ->					
Decision Support & Health Literacy	Passive Info, Discretionary Expenses, Rx, ER, D-X-L	Personal Health Mgmt, info with access incentives	Health & Perform. Info, Integrated Health & Work Data	Arrive in time information Information therapy, Targeted messaging	Friendship Pods, Wisemen, Sharing Circles, Social networks
Year ->					
Incentive, Rewards, Penalties	Cash, Tickets, Gift Cards, Trinkets,	Health Incentive Accts, Activity Incentives	Non-health corporate metric driven incentives	Personal Develop. Plan Incentives, Health Status	Psychic Rewards, Recognition, Honor, Respect, Love
Year ->					

The implementation process should assess what the organizational needs are, if solution providers are sufficiently capable of providing the needed services, and if new technologies are developing or likely to develop that would allow for better sequencing of actions.

The long term implementation plan will be an iterative process. A plan cannot implement a later generation concept until the vendors provide effective programs within that generation. But, vendors will not fully develop later generation programs until employers are ready to purchase such products. As in any free-market development, new leading edge vendors are building advanced generation solutions. They are creating a brand and loyal client base that once successful will typically merge or be acquired by larger capitalized companies.

The model for implementing HC recognizes several key issues:

1. Insurers/TPAs best value is providing a network of discounted care providers, and supplying a system to efficiently reimburse those providers.
2. There are multiple services and activities that need coordination and a level of "inter-operability".
3. A General Manager can coordinate the multiple services - A general manager may be the organization's HR department, an insurer/TPA, or an independent 3rd party.
4. A Private Exchange can operate as a general manager and coordinate multiple services - Private exchanges are run by consultants, technology companies, insurers, and others.
5. The coordinator of services should have a data warehouse that can gather and analyze information on each service provided
6. The coordinator of services should have a process for transforming analyzed data into actionable information to improve or change the services provided.

Video 117

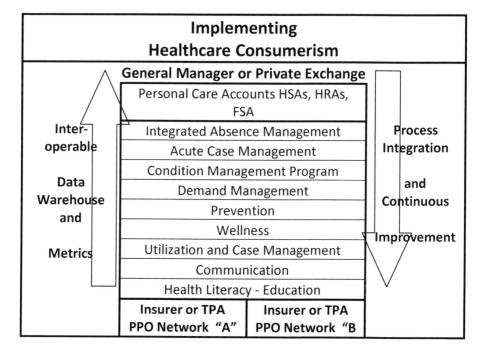

The secret to success is the cooperation and synergy between components supporting the organizational strategies.

In many cases, the general manager providing overall coordination, will be a true partner who provides several key services including: enrollment, personal care account processing, and condition management support. Some have suggested a "general contractor" could function in the coordinating role. The difference between a "general manager" and a "general contractor" is that a general manager only provides the coordination of services without providing any of the key service elements.

The option chosen may depend on the size of your organization and the size of the administrative budget. For organizations of fewer than 5000 employees, an integrated approach offered by insurers/TPAs may be the easiest option. Based upon focus group discussions with 20 of the Fortune 100 companies, the consensus was to engage an outside trusted 3rd party to act as a partner performing as a "general manager."

Understanding Healthcare Consumerism

The large organizations want to retain their data and reserve the right to change insurance carriers and networks at any time.

Below is a partial list of care support programs and services that are offered to plans and plan members. Depending on the organization and its strategic needs, some vendors will lower costs and improve care and some will only increase costs.

Implementing the myriad of available programs will prove challenging for any coordinating service provider.

Each organization is different with different needs. Technology advances are allowing cost effective new services online that appeal to younger plan members and making services more convenient with more choices.

HC Care Support Programs and Services		
Prescription Drug Info **Evidence Based Medicine** - Medical Care Guidelines - Health Library **Self-care Mgmt Info** **Condition/Disease Mgmt** - Condition Specific Tools - Chronic Wellness - Persistent Recovery - Voluntary Participation - Voluntary Incentives - Mandatory Participation - Mandatory Incentive Based **Health & Performance** - Population Mgmt - Case Mgmt - Cost & Quality Mgmt	**Stress Mgmt** - Assessment Tools - Self-help Tools **Depression Screening** **Preventive Care- Lifestyle** - Lifestyle - Nutrition - Fitness - Personal Health Mgmt **Preventive Care- Clinical** - Immunizations - Hypertension Screening - Cholesterol Testing - Mammograms - Pap Smears - Blood Pressure Checks - Colorectal Testing - Diabetes Testing - Osteoporosis Testing - Chlamydia Tests	**Wellness** - Online News - Social Networking **Early Intervention** **Safety** **Pre-Natal** **Well Baby Care** **New Mom Programs** **Medical Services** **Support** - Frequently Asked Questions - Inpatient preparation - Outpatient Options **Provider Cost/Quality Info** - Provider incentives **Centers of Excellences** - Regional Centers of Quality

In addition to the above listed care support programs, there are a myriad of decision support programs. These health literacy and decision support programs include: basic plan design information, personal benefit support programs, health management guidance, provider selection comparisons, and care support. Clearly, the challenge is to determine which programs will be of value to an organization and how to effectively coordinate and integrate the plethora of services. In the end HC is about engagement and changing behaviors.

Healthcare Consumerism Health Literacy & Decision Support Tools	
Provider Selection Support - Physician Quality Comparisons - Physician Cost Comparisons - Hospital Quality Comparisons - Hospital Cost Comparisons **Personal Benefit Support** - Plan Comparison Cost Estimator - Account Balance - On-line Claims Inquiry - Summary Plan Description - Appeals Info **Care Support** - On-line Provider Directory - Provider Scheduling - On-line Prescription Drug Support - 24/7 Nurse Line - Telemedicine	**Personal Health Management** - Health Risk Appraisals - Health & Wellness Info - Targeted Health Content - Medical Record, History - Health Coach - Wearables **Basic Design Information** - HRA Fund Accounting - HAS Fund Accounting - Underlying PPO Plan Design - Wellness, Wellbeing Benefits - Disease and/or Medical Mgmt - Debit/Credit Card

HC is a powerful concept that requires thoughtful and effective implementation. HC in its many forms is a mega-trend that will only improve over time. The U.S. healthcare system and insurance industry must change to meet new demands for choice, convenience, and access to affordable care.

As we move into the post-ACA era, HC will be center stage. Consumer-centered health insurance and patient-centered healthcare will merge into the world of HC options.

Based upon an analysis by Healthcare Visions. Inc. the following chart shows how HC concepts have been adopted and vary by size of organization .

Healthcare Consumerism Market Penetration					
Percentage of Employer's in 2017 Offering Major Features of Healthcare Consumerism by Group Size					
Building Blocks	* All Emp'rs	Small Emp'rs 100-500	Mid-Size Emp'rs 500-1K	Large Emp'rs 1k-5k	Jumbo Emp'rs >5,000
Savings Accts HSAs, HRAs	25%	35%	45%	60%	70%
Health Mgmt	25%	45%	60%	75%	85%
Condition Mgmt	25%	30%	50%	65%	80%
Health Literacy	15%	20%	40%	55%	70%
Incentives	20%	35%	45%	60%	75%
Source: Estimates based on overview of surveys reviewed by the Institute for Healthcare Consumerism. * "All Employers" column includes groups under 100 employees.					

2017 and Beyond – HC continues to evolve. New care models are developing from tele-health, m-health, direct payment, concierge services, and bundled services to Accountable Care Organizations.

We are shifting emphasis from health insurance reform to healthcare reform. We also see a shift from a focus on health to a desire for productive longevity.

Science, genomics, technology, and social media will likely influence the course of future health products and healthcare services. Governmental laws and regulations will form the basis for change and opportunities. Government laws and regulations can speed up or slow down the expansion of Healthcare Consumerism, but it cannot stop a megatrend.

Appendix A

The Development of
Healthcare Consumerism
in the United States

Key Moments in Modern U.S. Healthcare

In the United States, the federal government left health insurance matters to the States up until the early 20th century. The States, in turn, left health insurance up to private and voluntary programs. Here are key moments that formed the legal and market forces leading to Healthcare Consumerism.

1. 1920-30s - Blue Cross & Blue Shield: In 1929 Baylor University's health care facilities started the first insurance program in the U.S. for teachers in the Dallas area. During the depression years when most could not afford a hospital stay, a new financing system was adopted with a fixed cost (premium) that was paid for with a guarantee of limited number of hospital days. This became Blue Cross (BC). Following the lead of hospitals, Blue Shield (BS) was developed by employers in lumber and mining camps of the Pacific Northwest to provide medical care by paying monthly fees to groups of physicians. In 1939, the first official Blue Shield Plan was founded in California. Ultimately BC and BS joined to become dominant players in the U.S. health insurance industry.

2. 1944 – Public Service Act: The Public Health Service Act was enacted in 1944. It gave the United States Public Health Service responsibility for preventing the introduction, transmission and spread of communicable diseases from foreign countries into the United States.

3. 1940s - Employer-based Health Insurance: During the 2nd World War, wage and price controls were placed on American employers. To compete for workers, companies began to offer health benefits, giving rise to the employer-based system.

4. 1965 – Medicare & Medicaid: In 1965, President Johnson signed the Medicare and Medicaid programs into law, providing comprehensive, low-cost health insurance coverage to the elderly and low income.

5. 1974 - ERISA: The Employee Retirement Income Security Act of 1974 (ERISA) was enacted September 2, 1974. While originally thought to cover only retirement plans, subsequent court cases established self-insured health plans under ERISA to be exempt from state insurance laws. Self-insured plans shift the risk of plan solvency from insurance companies to employers. These rulings started the movement towards widely used self-insured plans that use insurers and TPAs as administrators. Subsequent amendments to ERISA include:

a. The Consolidated Omnibus Budget Reconciliation Act of 1985 (COBRA) which provides some employees and beneficiaries with the right to continue their coverage under an employer-sponsored group health benefit plan for a limited time after the occurrence of certain events that would otherwise cause termination of such coverage.

b. The Health Insurance Portability and Accountability Act of 1996 (HIPAA) prohibits a health benefit plan from refusing to cover an employee's pre-existing medical conditions in some circumstances. It also bars health benefit plans from certain types of discrimination on the basis of health status, genetic information, or disability.

c. Other relevant amendments to ERISA include the Newborns' and Mothers' Health Protection Act, the Mental Health Parity Act, and the Women's Health and Cancer Rights Act.

6. 1978 – Flexible Spending Arrangements: This is the first account based option for employee contributions. However, it included a use-it-or-lose-it provision for unspent funds at the end of a calendar year. Allowed by Treasury In 1978, Flexible Spending Accounts provide for employees to have their compensation reduced by an amount necessary to cover certain fixed benefit costs and non-fixed benefit costs with pre-tax dollars rather than after-tax dollars. Eligible benefit costs include health insurance premiums, dependent care, dental care, vision care, other services not reimburse by the regular health plan, etc.

7. 1973 - HMO Act: It was the first step in creating a "Managed Care" system. Enacted December 29, 1973, the federal HMO Act provided for a trial program to promote and encourage the development of HMOs. The HMO Act amended the 1944 Public Health Service Act.

8. 1970-80s – PPOs/EPOs: This was the first step in creating proprietary insurance owned provider discounted networks. In the 1970s, employers began using preferred-provider organizations (PPOs). PPOs steer employees to cooperating doctors and hospitals that have agreed to a predetermined discount reimbursement for services provided. Various forms of PPOs were created, including Exclusive Provider Organizations (EPOs) that were very limited generally localized networks of hospitals.

9. 1983 – DRGs: This was the first phase of establishing a bundled payment for hospital services. On October 1, 1983, Medicare's new Prospective Payment System (PPS) became effective for payment of services to hospitals. According to this payment scheme, hospitals are paid a fixed amount per patient discharge. The rate of reimbursement will be based on Diagnosis Related Groups, a classification of 467 illness categories. For Medicare, the Prospective Payment System replaces the fee-for-service plan in which the payment is cost-based and retrospectively determined following treatment.

10. 1990s – Hospital Owned HMO's: This was the first movement towards provider risk-bearing through owned insurance companies. During the mid-1990s, starting hospital owned HMOs was a managed case growth industry. New opportunities were opening to serve employers, state Medicaid programs and seniors on Medicare. Hospitals concluded that the best way to regain some of the economic power they had lost to HMOs was to try and play the same game. From 1995 to 1997, literally dozens of HMOs were formed (or acquired in a few cases) by hospital organizations.

11. 1996 - Medical Savings Accounts (MSA) – The MSA must be coupled with a high-deductible health plan (HDHP). This is first form of Consumer-Driven Healthcare. Pat Rooney, founder and president of Golden Rule Insurance Company was instrumental in the 1996 passage of Medical Savings Account (MSA) pilot program that allows for tax-free contributions to a medical savings account. It was passed as a part of the Health Insurance Portability and Accountability Act (HIPAA) in 1996.

12. 2002 - Health Reimbursement Arrangements (HRA): HRAs were the first non-pilot savings accounts option that spurred the initial Consumer-Driven Healthcare Movement. While only employer allotments were allowed, this is the first time a continuous carry forward of an account was allowed. An HRA is an arrangement that: (1) is funded solely by the employer, (2) reimburses the employee for medical care expenses incurred by the employee and the employee's spouse and dependents and, (3) provides reimbursements up to a maximum dollar amount for a coverage period and any unused portion of the maximum dollar amount at the end of a coverage period is carried forward to increase the maximum reimbursement amount in subsequent coverage periods.

13. 2003 – Health Savings Accounts (HSA): HSAs are the first to financially empower employees with medical dollars to spend in addition to coverage under High Deductible Health Plans. HSAs continued a trend of employee empowerment and the movement to Consumer-Driven Healthcare. In December of 2003, the Medicare Modernization Act (MMA) prescription drug bill was passed that also included Health Savings Accounts. HSAs are real dollars put into savings accounts and owned by employees. Employers, employers, and even other third parties can contribute triple tax advantaged dollars into an HSA (tax deductible, tax free accumulation, and non-taxed qualified withdrawals).

14. 2000s - Healthcare Consumerism: Healthcare Consumerism is a term reflecting most of HC, but has a connotation relating to the purchase of insurance more than the interaction with the delivery of care. It is a natural market extension of account-based plans. As account-based plans, including HRAs and HSAs, gained favor in reducing costs, additional support services surfaced to expand on the pure account-based plan designs. Wellness initiatives, disease management, incentives and rewards, and health education allowed for effective engagement of plan members in making better informed health and healthcare decisions.

15. 2010 – The ACA & Health Marketplaces: The development of Healthcare Consumerism was accelerated by the Patient Protection and Affordable Care Act that was signed into law on March 20, 2010. The ACA established comprehensive health insurance reforms, including the creation of health insurance marketplaces (also called health exchanges). The ACA mandated coverages have highlighted the relative affordability of HSA High Deductible Health Plans. The Health Marketplaces, sometimes under employer fixed defined contribution financing, offer individuals more choice of coverages. Healthcare Consumerism has continued to grow and flourish under the ACA.

16. 2017+: Patient-Centered Healthcare Consumerism – As we move from "health insurance reform" to actual "healthcare reform" the term Patient-Centered Healthcare Consumerism will become more prevalent. In most surveys on healthcare, individuals do not see themselves as consumers but as patients. As the ACA is repealed, replaced or at least substantially changed, the basis of change will be based on the more inclusive concepts of patient centered care. New care models will develop with lower cost, greater convenience, and higher quality. Tele-health, direct payment, concierge services, bundled services, and IoTs will provide more personalized services.

As we shift emphasis from health insurance reform to healthcare reform, we will also see a shift from health and healthcare to a goal of productive longevity. Science, genomics, technology, and social media will influence the course of future healthcare products and care. Governmental laws and regulations will form the basis for change and opportunities. Government laws and regulations can speed up or slow down the expansion of Patient-Centered Healthcare Consumerism, but cannot stop it as a megatrend.

Appendix B

Generation 6 ?

Whenever I teach a course based on the materials presented in this book, I inevitably am asked what is coming next? What is likely to be the sixth generation? I regularly respond that the model and ideas presented are not think tank or academic ideas. So, the 6th generation will appear as a response to various market and industry forces.

Of course, there are two main forces supporting new products and services. First, free market entrepreneurs are using new technologies, expanded acceptance of social media products, big data platforms, and creative combinations of existing ideas. Second, government laws and regulations determine the legal framework that allows or disallows certain products or services.

The generations presented in this book were developed only after substantial evidence that a full range of products were already available or in some instances would be possible with potential legislation or accommodating regulations.

The potential for a game changing new generation of HC may come from the development of the "Internet of Things" (IoTs). The promise of new technologies to change how insurance is purchased (e.g. on-line), how health is maintained (e.g. wearables), how benefits are used (e.g patient-centered), and how care is delivered (e.g. personal health records, telemedicine).

A definition of Health IoT is a network of appliances and activities connected through the Internet. They contain embedded technology to collect results, monitor, and report on the personalized health and healthcare status to the individual and/or care providers. When information flows and data can be inter-related and analyzed in real time, it changes how and where decisions are made, and who makes them.

So, watch closely as personal and enterprise solutions embrace the IoT concepts, the public acceptance of the products and services, and the legal regulatory changes needed to facilitate this brave new world. Only with public acceptance and adoption will we be able to see more clearly if this or another trend will emerge as a sixth generation of HC.

Appendix C

5 Minute Video Lessons Supporting
Healthcare Consumerism

If you are reading this video-text in electronic form, the videos are a simple click on the "video options" found throughout the book. If you are reading this book in paper copy, you will need to access the internet through your PC, iPad, phone, or other mobile device. QR codes for video links are generally found at the end of each chapter. You will also find videos at www.hcbookvideos.com

Video Link	Topic
CHCC 101	Principles, Vision, Strategies
CHCC 102	Creating Real Change
CHCC 103	Defining Healthcare Consumerism
CHCC 104	Basic Requirements of Healthcare Consumerism
CHCC 105	Choices with Healthcare Consumerism
CHCC 106	The Patient-Provider Relationship
CHCC 107	Healthcare Consumerism Generation 1&2
CHCC 108	Healthcare Consumerism Generation 3
CHCC 109	Healthcare Consumerism Generation 4
CHCC 110	The Healthcare Consumerism Grid
CHCC 111	Healthcare Consumerism Generation 5
CHCC 112	HRAs & HSAs
CHCC 113	Health & Condition Management
CHCC 114	Determinants of Health
CHCC 115	Stress Management
CHCC 116	Personalized Healthcare
CHCC 117	Implementing Healthcare Consumerism
CHCC 118	Potential Savings
CHCC 119	Consumerism & Venture Capital
CHCC 120	Consumerism & Health Exchanges

Similar videos have been interspersed throughout the text of this book and placed in the appropriate location related to the topic (not necessarily in the order listed above).

ABOUT THE AUTHOR

Ronald E. Bachman FSA, MAAA, CHC
President & CEO, Healthcare Visions

Ronald E. Bachman has been at the center of U.S. health care transformation, advancing free market consumer-based solutions to lower the number of uninsureds, improve mental health coverage, and advance employer introductions of healthcare consumerism. Currently he is the President and CEO of Healthcare Visions, a thought leadership firm dedicated to advancing ideas and policy initiatives that are impacting the U.S. health care market.

Bachman has been a Senior Fellow of the National Center for Policy Analysis, the Wye River Group on Health, the Center for Health Transformation, and the Georgia Public Policy Foundation (GPPF). He is an Adviser to the Goodman Policy Institute. As an actuary, he has extensive experience in healthcare strategy for payers, providers and employers. Ron has been Chairman of the Editorial Advisory Board for Field Media and the Institute for Healthcare Consumerism. Bachman is on advisory boards for HINRI Labs and Jacobs Ladder Autism Center. He has also served on boards for Skyland Trail, Bryan University, and the Georgia Charity Care Network.

Formerly, Bachman was a principal with PricewaterhouseCoopers, where he consulted to a broad range of clients including: employers, HMOs, hospitals, physicians, indemnity carriers, BlueCross BlueShield plans, as well as State and Federal Agency clients.

Over the years Bachman has worked on health policy issues and market transformation ideas. He worked closely with the Bush White House and Treasury on the language and principles of the 2002 Health Reimbursement Arrangement (HRA) guidelines and provided policy input on Health Savings Accounts (HSA).

Working across the political aisle Ron has worked with Speaker Newt Gingrich, the Carter Center, Senator Ted Kennedy, and Senator Paul Wellstone on mental health issues. He testified in over 30 states and before Congress in support of mental health parity. He has served as a designated expert on actuarial issues to the Centers for Medicare and Medicaid Services (CMS), the Congressional Research Service (CRS), the Congressional Budget Office (CBO), the Department of Labor (DOL), the National Institute of Mental Health (NIMH), the Substance Abuse and Mental Health Services Administration (SAMHSA) and several members of Congress.

Ron is a graduate of Georgia Tech with a BS in Applied Mathematics and has a M.A.S. from Georgia State University. A sampling of his articles include: "Consumer-Driven Healthcare – The Future is Now", "Giving Patients More Control", "An Employer's Guide to Patient-Directed Healthcare Benefits", "An Employer's Guide to Pharmaceutical Benefits", "A Legislator's Guide to Creating an HSA State", "Lowering the Uninsured During an Economic Down Turn", "An American Solution to Healthcare", "Depression is Bottom Line Issue – If CEO's Only Knew", "Corporate Readiness for Healthcare Consumerism", and "Web 2.0 and the Next Generation of Healthcare Consumerism."

After the Book

After reading the book you may want to go into greater depth and extend your knowledge of Healthcare Consumerism. You are now ready to take the ultimate challenge of learning more and getting certified as a real expert on Healthcare Consumerism.

The FREE IHC University website gives you more on Healthcare Consumerism and allows you to earn the designation "Certified in Healthcare Consumerism" (CHC) that you can place after your name on business cards and on your letter head.

Register NOW for Taking the CHC Exam: Passing this test with an 80% or better score will earn you the CHC designation and a certification trophy for passing.

How to take the CHC Exam
Simply go to the CHC Certification section on the website or Click or paste the www.ihcuniversity.com URL into your web browser or use your iphone to read the QR Code below:

HC Videos   CHC Certification   IHC University

How to earn the CHC Certification
To receive the certification you will need to take the exam, fill out the answer sheet (supplied at the website), and submit your answers by email to ronbachman@healthcarevisions.net or snail mail to:

IHC University
200 Gulf Shore Dr.
Unit 521
Destin, Florida 32541

Additional Books: You can also purchase additional copies at:
www.IHCUniversity.com

Made in the USA
Columbia, SC
09 September 2017